ESCAPING
SPIRITUAL OBLIVION
RECLAIMING TRUE CONSCIOUSNESS

Anthony Benjamin Cosenza, Ph.D.

ESCAPING SPIRITUAL OBLIVION
RECLAIMING TRUE CONSCIOUSNESS

iUniverse books may be ordered through booksellers or by contacting:

iUniverse
1663 Liberty Drive
Bloomington, IN 47403
www.iuniverse.com
844-349-9409

Because of the dynamic nature of the Internet, any web addresses or links contained in this book may have changed since publication and may no longer be valid. The views expressed in this work are solely those of the author and do not necessarily reflect the views of the publisher, and the publisher hereby disclaims any responsibility for them.

Free Stock Images on the book cover and back cover are from Pixabay.

All Scriptures used, unless otherwise indicated, are taken from the King James Version of The Bible. Explanatory insertions of scripture verses by the author are enclosed in brackets [].

ISBN: 978-1-6632-5838-0 (sc)
ISBN: 978-1-6632-5837-3 (e)

Library of Congress Control Number: 2024902700

Print information available on the last page.

iUniverse rev. date: 04/09/2024

DEDICATION

This book is dedicated to all of those spiritual leaders and counselors who endeavored to search for truth concerning the nature of crises across religion, science and philosophy.

ACKNOWLEDGEMENTS

I am especially grateful to Dr. Anthony Portafoglio for his continued support of my work on spiritual consciousness and growth in grace.

CONTENTS

Introduction...xv

Section 1: True Consciousness.. 1

Part I: Origin of Spiritual Consciousness.............................. 3

1.   False Thinking, Flawed Consciousness........................... 5
2.   Spiritual Oblivion.. 7
3.   Grace and Consciousness..11
4.   Inherent Spiritual Consciousness 13

Part II: Consciousness of Spiritual Values...........................17

5.   Spiritual Worship Values 19
6.   Nine Manifestations of Holy Spirit........................... 24

Part III: Spiritual Oblivion Demonstrated........................... 29

7.   Spiritual Oblivion: A Distortion of Worship Values........... 33
8.   Cause and Effect of Man's Problems........................... 36
9.   Conversion: A Spiritual Awakening 40
10. Spiritual Man's Return to Oblivion 45
11. Worship Oblivion.. 48

Part IV: Spiritual Dimensions of Worship Oblivion 53

12. OB #1: Love Oblivion 55
13. Spiritually Conscious Love 60
14. OB #2: Need/Sufficiency Oblivion............................. 65

15. OB #3: Discerning Oblivion.................................... 71

16. Book of Acts and Discerning of Spirits 76

17. OB #4: Conversation Oblivion 80

18. Listening for an Answer...................................... 84

19. Spiritually Based Prayer 88

20. Speaking in Tongues 92

Part V: Worship Oblivion of The Word of God 95

21. OB #5: Incongruence Oblivion 97

22. OB #6: Integrity Oblivion 102

23. OB #7: Research Oblivion 108

Part VI: Worship Oblivion of One's Spiritual Worth.......... 115

24. OB #8: Condemnation Oblivion 117

25. OB #9: Righteousness Oblivion.............................. 123

26. Perceived Unrighteousness.................................. 127

27. OB #10: Hope Oblivion 131

28. OB #11: Example/comparison Oblivion........................ 138

Part VII: From Oblivion to Consciousness.................... 147

29. Step One: Accept Our Inherent Spiritual Consciousness 151

30. Step Two: Identify Oblivion Subtypes 154

31. Step Three: Develop Spiritually Conscious Goals........... 159

32. Step Four: Evaluate Values of Worship 164

33. Step Five: Use the Principle of Spiritual Valorization 170

34. Step Six: Evaluate Christ-centered Verses On Spiritual Worth 173

Part VIII: The Balance of Consciousness 179

35. Maintaining Spiritual Balance 181
36. Deceptions and Balances 186

Epilogue 189
Appendix A 193
References 197

Part VIII. The Politics of Conversation 377

9. Meanings Settled and Unsettled 381
10. Exceptions and Effects ....

Epilogue 390
Appendix 393
References 399

SIGNIFICANT LIFE ALTERING QUESTIONS
REGARDING TRUE CONSCIOUSNESS AND OBLIVION

- ☐ *What is spiritual consciousness?*
- ☐ *When and how did spiritual consciousness begin?*
- ☐ *Is there only one true consciousness?*
- ☐ *Can one lose spiritual consciousness but not the spiritual nature created by God?*

- ☐ *How and why do we lose levels of spiritual consciousness and become spiritually oblivious?*
- ☐ *Do errors in true spiritual worship result in continued spiritual oblivion?*

- ☐ *How does God help us to maintain and reclaim the spiritual consciousness that we inherently are meant to manifest?*
- ☐ *Are there true spiritual dimensions of worship that result in increased spiritual consciousness?*
- ☐ *Are grace and prayer vital for continued consciousness?*

INTRODUCTION

For the most part, we live a life of spiritual oblivion, unaware of the reality of the One True God who is Spirit. Enraptured by a material world where everything is perceived as matter and not spirit, we have become confused by or disinterested in spiritual understanding and consciousness. Consequently, we remain totally unaware that we are spiritual beings already created in God's image.

> Genesis 1:27:
> So God created man in his own image [Spirit], in the image of God created he him; male and female created he them.

> John 4:24:
> God is a Spirit: and they that worship him must worship him in spirit and in truth.

We may be interested in human consciousness or awareness so as to function well here and now both personally and interpersonally. But human consciousness does not provide the answers and wholeness we need to have a life that is more than abundant. We live and think in and of a world of matter and do not realize or show concern that matter is not spirit. In fact, we will find that Matter and Spirit are complete opposites. The Word of God has lost spiritual understanding because we intellectualize the world and our research of the Word. More often then not, the world has taught us that we are human beings, made of matter.

In the Bible, early man has been portrayed as having lost spirit because of disobedience to God. Yet, God is Spirit and He can only relate to spirit.

When Adam disobeyed God in the Garden of Eden, God was still able to talk with him. It was not that Adam lost spirit. If that were so, as a spiritual being, he would no longer exist. By his loss of a sense of spiritual consciousness, he became blinded and oblivious to spiritual matters.

Dr. Cosenza's seventh book, *Escaping Spiritual Oblivion*, represents a 50-year research investigation into value clarification counseling, crisis intervention and the true meanings of spiritual consciousness and spiritual oblivion. In current times of significant personal, community and worldly dysfunctions, the author examines truths and misconceptions that affect our understanding of true spiritual causes and effects of flawed mortal conditions.

Dr. Cosenza's latest work offers an expanded biblical study of the deeper dimensions of worship and how it significantly relates to states of consciousness and oblivion. Many of the author's ideas and research evolved over time and were adapted, revised, and modified from his previous six books related to biblically based counseling and crisis resolution.

The stunning truth unlocked in *Escaping Spiritual Oblivion* is that all of mortal man's present, past and future critical conditions are solely related to "spiritual worship values" and errors in spiritual understanding of God as the One who is all knowing, all truth, all life, all loving, all powerful and all Spirit. He is the only one to be worshipped. Personal or worldly disturbances of life continue because of man's mistaken mortal thoughts and worldly mental habit patterns regarding who, what and how to worship. Spiritual truth concerning *worship* is expressed in the Gospel of John.

John 4:23:

But the hour cometh, and now is, when the true worshippers shall worship the Father in spirit and in truth: for the Father seeketh such to worship him.

True worship of God involves both spirit and truth; in other words, "truthful spirit" or "spiritual truth." Errors in worship include spiritual misunderstanding of the workings of the Spirit of God, spiritual blindness concerning the true Word of God and ignorance or rejection of our true inherent nature as spiritual beings.

False beliefs or refusal to accept what God thinks of us and how He values us will determine the course and outcome of our openness to spiritual consciousness.

Man may have some sense of whom and how to highly value God (*worship*), but lacks spiritual knowledge of the Word of God and/or the truth about his spiritual value through God. In this case, man may believe that Almighty God is to be worshipped, but does he really know God or the truth about himself from the inspired Word?

Man may also study and gain increasing spiritual understanding of the Scriptures, but does he know or accept how to spiritually honor God or appreciate that he is created in God's image?

Man may be spiritually aware of his inherent Divine nature, but he does not know or recognize how to worship spiritually through an understanding of the Word of God.

Spiritual man (the man with gracious spiritual consciousness of God and the things of the Spirit) needs to remain free of worldly crises. Mortal or natural man (five-sense man without spiritual consciousness of God) already is in crises and will remain so until he turns to God for truth, enlightenment, and love. Jesus was so accurate when he said, "Ye do err, not knowing the scriptures, nor the power of God (Matthew 22:29 (b))." We sustain major errors in mental patterns and a resulting crisis when we do not spiritually know the Word of God or the power of God through spiritual consciousness of worship.

To explore effective solutions to mortal problems, first we need to identify biblically specific worship values of consciousness. **Spiritual oblivion** is the result of continued inaccurate or blinded spiritual consciousness of worship. Once these types are known and goals are developed, we pursue a process that this book describes as *spiritual valorization* (Cosenza, 2006). This approach provides a bombardment of biblically based values, which include evaluating our thinking and habits regarding worship in the spirit through a spiritual sense of the Word of God and a fuller conception of our true spiritual identity. Through continued *doctrine, reproof* and *correction* of our mental patterns concerning these worship values of consciousness, we come to spiritually understand, withstand, develop short and long-term strategies, and ultimately negate the reality of mortal critical conditions.

> *Who would have imagined that the secret to a deeper*
> *understanding and intervention in the world would*
> *be found solely in the realm of spiritual consciousness?*

SECTION ONE
TRUE CONSCIOUSNESS

True consciousness is completely and totally spiritual.

All other displays of consciousness are false illusions, unrealities, unreal dreams and errors in one's mortal mind and thoughts based upon material information from a five-senses world. Spiritual consciousness does not co-mingle or exist with matter or some other level or class of consciousness. In the spiritual realm, there is no competing force or power that is beyond God, the Father of Jesus Christ. In this realm, there is no matter, materialism, sickness, evil or death. There is no other greater power than God. The First Book of Genesis captures the greatness and wonder of God's "good works".

> Genesis 1:31(a):
> And God saw everything that he had made and it
> was good.

Ideas of "mortal man" and "human consciousness" evolved from certain misguided beliefs in The Bible, Genesis 2, where man is falsely perceived as incomplete, lost, without spirit, worth-less, valueless, and fallen from grace.

Spiritual consciousness is not human consciousness.

It is not a psychological concept such as Freud's "unconscious" or "subconscious." The conscious and subconscious dimensions of Freudian or psychological consciousness are in the same category as human or mortal consciousness. Both levels of consciousness involve thoughts, beliefs, facts and experiences that have been or can be retrieved by mortal man in the natural world. Freud's "unconscious" is still in the real of the mortal mind because its specific content contains negative mortal thoughts and the human circumstances associated with them.

PART I
ORIGIN OF SPIRITUAL CONSCIOUSNESS

Spiritual consciousness is the awareness of
God's spiritual truth, light and love.

In the beginning, God created the heavens and the earth (Gen. 1:1). God is Spirit (John 4:4). God is light (I John 1:5). God is love (I John 4:8). Consciousness of these three spiritual ideas enlightens our understanding of the meaning of truth, life and love. There was no real spiritual consciousness before God created it. There is no other source for consciousness except God.

"So-called consciousness," as described by most authors, involves levels of depth of understanding regarding the material world and our mortal sense of being in this world now, in this day and time. Mortal consciousness is a dream state of material life based upon human intelligence, perceptions and viewpoint. This material dream state includes ideas of extrasensory information and some archetype of nature.

> *Outside of God, there is darkness, regardless of what*
> *terms of enlightenment are explored, explained or*
> *apparently demonstrated.*

"...the five physical senses are simply the manifested beliefs of mortal mind, which affirm that life, substance, and intelligence are material, instead of spiritual. These false beliefs and their products constitute the flesh, and the flesh wars against Spirit." Excerpt From: Mary Baker Eddy. "Science and Health with Key to the Scriptures (Authorized Edition)." Apple Books. https://books.apple.com/us/book/science-and-health-with-key-to-the/id441922830

1

FALSE THINKING, FLAWED CONSCIOUSNESS

"Every system of human philosophy, doctrine, and medicine is more or less infected with the pantheistic belief that there is mind in matter; but this belief contradicts alike revelation and right reasoning. "(Excerpt From: Mary Baker Eddy. "Science and Health with Key to the Scriptures (Authorized Edition)." Apple Books. https://books.apple.com/us/book/science-and-health-with-key-to-the/id441922830n

Many authors speak of having a spiritual nature and being spiritually attuned, but they avoid a discussion or explanation of God, how He came to create spiritual consciousness, and how Jesus Christ and the Holy Spirit provided the avenues of enriched awareness necessary to manifest the spiritual power that can heal. The term "Christ consciousness" suspends the truth concerning Jesus Christ and the impact of the Holy Spirit in manifesting spiritual intuition. Because of this lack of exploration, the only other key that is provided nowadays is "meditation," which includes various meanings and applications of levels of consciousness and whether or not they are truly spirit based.

Human consciousness of the material world around us is unreal because it is oblivious to spiritual meaning and understanding. Human consciousness is unreal versus spiritual consciousness, which is real and eternal.

The world teaches that consciousness is the awareness of the NOW, of BEING, of TRUTH. What BEING? What is NOW? What is TRUTH?

The Bible says that Jesus Christ is truth (John 14:8), the Word of God is truth (John 17:17), and the Holy Spirit provides truth (John 16:13).

When the literature discusses "God consciousness," it is still referring to self-awareness of one's being but with little cognizance as to how God Himself graciously provides spiritual awareness. We need to know how Jesus Christ enlarges that awareness and how the manifestations of Holy Spirit operate to demonstrate spiritual power. In various writings of God-consciousness, there is little reference to the worship of God, the significance of the Word of God, and the realities of how God helps us to manifest our spiritual worth through the Holy Spirit.

"Evil thinking is the source of all wrong consciousness." Night dreams are not real but illusions. The waking world is also an illusion and a counterfeit that cloaks us from spiritual knowledge, understanding and insight. There are night dreams and awakened dreams, none of which are true spiritual consciousness because they are based upon matter and the material world. The opposite of spiritual consciousness is oblivion; death; being asleep, a dream state. When what we erroneously term as the five physical senses, we are misdirected. They are simply the manifested beliefs of mortal mind, which affirm that life, substance, and intelligence are material, instead of spiritual. These false beliefs and their products constitute the flesh, and the flesh wars against Spirit." (Excerpt From: Mary Baker Eddy. "Science and Health with Key to the Scriptures (Authorized Edition)." Apple Books. https://books.apple.com/us/book/science-and-health-with-key-to-the/id441922830

2

SPIRITUAL OBLIVION

Spiritual consciousness is the opposite of spiritual oblivion.

True spiritual consciousness is the gracious awareness of true spiritual worship through (1) spiritual love and praise of the one true God, (2) a spiritual understanding of the Word of God (and Christ as the Word of God in the flesh), and (3) spiritual understanding that we are spiritual beings created in His (God's) image, which is Spirit.

> John 4:4:
> God is Spirit and they that worship Him must worship him in spirit and in truth.

> Philippians 3:3:
> For we are the circumcision, which worship God in Spirit, rejoice [by rejoicing] in Christ Jesus, and have [having] no confidence in the flesh.

The key to increased spiritual consciousness is WORSHIP of the one true God who is Spirit. This worship comes through a spiritual understanding of truth and involves rejoicing in the resurrected Christ, and giving no credit to materialism or matter. There is only one power and that is God. God is truth, His Word is truth, Jesus Christ is the way, the truth and the life. Worship by Spirit includes prayer, spiritual dimensions of worship, knowing and operating the nine manifestations of spirit, operating the gifts of grace and operating the five spiritual gift ministries. The Spirit of God conveys truth to those who are conscious of spiritual matters.

Spiritual oblivion is the opposite of true spiritual consciousness.

Oblivion is an unawareness of the role of Spirit. It is a consciousness of matter and things of the world. Material or worldly consciousness has errors in or no thinking about the spiritual truths of Worship, Word-ship and worth-ship. It is a spiritual blindness of the grace to live and have our being in Him. Mortal man cannot receive or understand the spiritual things of God.

Spiritual oblivion can and will only include an awareness of matter and its effects without spiritual impact; it is the illusion of reality; it is a dream state with a focus on the now and a sense of being from a five-senses man perspective. Spiritual oblivion would be equivalent to man's material or five-sense consciousness. It is the absence or loss of spiritual consciousness. We need to grow in spiritual consciousness.

> Ephesians 1: 17-19:
> That the God of our Lord Jesus Christ, the Father of glory, may give unto you the spirit of wisdom and revelation in the knowledge of him:
> The eyes of your understanding being enlightened; that ye may know what is the hope of his calling, and what the riches of the glory who because of circumstances lost inheritance in the saints,
> And what is the exceeding greatness of his power to us-ward who believe, according to the working of his mighty power,

Colossians 1:9-10:

> For this cause we also, since the day we heard it, do not cease to pray for you, and to desire that ye might be filled with the knowledge of his will in all wisdom and spiritual understanding;

> That ye might walk worthy of the Lord unto all pleasing, being fruitful in every good work, and increasing in the knowledge of God;

The Word of God enhances consciousness and fills our hearts and mind with the ingredients of true spiritual worship, true Word, and the Christ Spirit within.

Loss of Spiritual Consciousness

There is a Biblical basis for spiritual consciousness, beginning in Genesis, Chapter 1. We are "created in His image (Gen. 1:26-27)." All was light; God separated the light from darkness. All He had done was good and completed (Gen. 1:31). Spiritual consciousness is an awareness of truth and error, an awakening from a dream.

In Genesis 2, there a picture presented as mortal man who because of circumstances spiritual consciousness lost his sense of spiritual consciousness (Genesis, Chapters 2 & 3). He remained a spiritual being with whom God who is Spirit (John 4:4) spoke. This loss of spiritual understanding was replaced by sin-consciousness, self-consciousness, and oblivion. Man became perceived as human, a mortal being, and not the spiritual being he was created to be in Genesis, Chapter 1. With this loss of a spiritual sense of consciousness or spiritual oblivion, mortal man (not God's spiritual being, made in His image) saw himself, believed and acted as though he were lost, fallen, unworthy and incomplete. This oblivion is comparable to spiritual death; spiritual unconsciousness; being asleep. If God is Spirit and Adam actually lost spirit as others have reported, how was God able to speak with Adam and reprove him?

Is there eternal oblivion? Not according to the Bible, since God made available ways for mortal man to increase his awareness and come to the knowledge of Him, His Word and our worth.

3

GRACE AND CONSCIOUSNESS

Ephesians 1:3-6:

Blessed be the God and Father of our Lord Jesus Christ, who has blessed us with every spiritual blessing in the heavenly places in Christ,

According as He hath chosen us in Him before the foundation of the world, that we should be holy and without blame before Him in love,

Having predestined us to adoption as sons by Jesus Christ to Himself, according to the good pleasure of His will,

To the praise of the glory of His grace, by which He made us accepted in the beloved.

All of God's grace, which is free unmerited favor, became available when he predestined for us before the foundation of the world that we should be holy and without blame. Grace is related to God's "election." Paul sees God as electing us before the creation of the world for the purpose of holiness and blamelessness. Election and grace are free. We can do nothing to deserve them.

Are there states of spiritual consciousness?

Some authors discuss "states of consciousness" but they are levels of consciousness of the world and our awareness of self and others in the world. These states have nothing to do with spiritual consciousness. They include man's opinions, beliefs, cultural and intellectual awareness, synthesizing, scientific thought, and inductive/deductive reasoning. Even the highest stage of consciousness still concludes man's inner perceptions of insight and intuition. Although this may be considered to be comparable to spiritual consciousness, it is still based on higher levels of man's thinking and perceiving internally.

God's grace and love continue to take us out of oblivion into the spiritual light.

God wants us to reclaim the spiritual consciousness He made available and created in His image. In the Old Testament, certain individuals such as Noah and Moses understood God's grace and consequently attained a heightened level of the spiritual awareness they were created to have and be. As a result, these individuals were able to operate the manifestations of the Holy Spirit except for *speaking in tongues*, which was manifested on the Day of Pentecost.

> Acts 2: 1-4:
> And when the day of Pentecost was fully come, they were all with one accord in one place.
> 2 And suddenly there came a sound from heaven as of a rushing mighty wind, and it filled all the house where they were sitting.
> 3 And there appeared unto them cloven tongues like as of fire, and it sat upon each of them.
> 4 And they were all filled with the Holy Ghost, and began to speak with other tongues, as the Spirit gave them utterance.

Consequently, these Old Testament and New Testament individuals had revelation from God through His Word of Knowledge and Word of Wisdom. They could heal and perform miracles that only God could reveal to them regarding how and what to do.

4

INHERENT SPIRITUAL CONSCIOUSNESS

Spiritual consciousness began with and by God. Spiritual consciousness is a deeper awareness of the meaning of true worship.

John 4:4:

We worship God in Spirit and in truth.

This consciousness involves a spiritual understanding of the omnipotence of God, the one true God, through inspired prayer, the operation of 'the nine manifestations of the Spirit" (I Cor. 12), the functioning of "the five gift ministries, and continued spiritual understanding of the written Word of God, His spoken Word and the Word "in the flesh" (Jesus Christ). This is the spiritual meaning of true spiritual worship.

"The three great verities of Spirit are omnipotence, omnipresence, omniscience, — Spirit possessing all power, filling all space, constituting all Science, — contradict forever the belief that matter can be actual. These eternal verities reveal primeval existence as the radiant reality of God's creation, in which all that He has made is pronounced by His wisdom good." Excerpt From: Mary Baker Eddy. "Science and Health with Key to the Scriptures (Authorized Edition)." Apple Books. https://books. apple.com/us/book/science-and-health-with-key-to-the/ id441922830

Consciousness Level #1: Knowing that God is Spirit and that we are created in His image, which is Spirit.

Spiritual consciousness is a continued moment-by-moment, here and now awakening to the true spiritual reality that all men and women are created in God's image, which is Spirit (Genesis 1:26-27). We have an eternal spiritual relationship with God that can never be lost or replaced. WE ARE SPIRITUAL AND ALWAYS WILL BE. This fundamental and primary level of awareness ultimately replaces long-held mortal awareness of sin-consciousness and self-consciousness.

Consciousness Level #2: A spiritual understanding that Jesus Christ brought us to a new level of love, truth and grace by his life, death, resurrection and the ascension.

Grace came with Jesus Christ. By his crucifixion and resurrection, he exhibited, enlightened and enlarged our consciousness to the power of Spirit over matter, the power of spiritual consciousness over mortal beliefs and thoughts. He overcame our false sense of sin-consciousness, unworthiness and self-consciousness. *In level 2, we spiritually come to understand and become aware of the Christ Spirit that was in Christ and now and always has been our divine spiritual nature as God's spiritual beings created in His image.* Through Jesus Christ, we gained a full level of man's true God-given consciousness. He proved the power of true consciousness to demonstrate the falsity of all evil and the reality of health and holiness. Jesus was the human messenger who came to bring the message of the Christ, the spiritual idea of God and man, which, as it is understood, illumines consciousness with the spiritual sense of Life wherein man is forever at-one with God.

Christ in you, the hope of glory (Colossians 1:27).

The past, present and future can only be spiritually understood through the accuracy and integrity of the Word of God concerning the Christ, to the point of living it. While here on earth, Jesus was the walking and talking Word with all of its demonstrations.

Consciousness Level #3: Knowledge and manifestation of God's spiritual love (I Cor. 13).

We have a spiritual awakening to the meaning of God's love and how to manifest it as true spiritual beings to others.

Consciousness Level #4: We learn how to operate the nine "manifestations of the Holy Spirit."

> I Corinthians 12:7-11:
>
> **7** But the manifestation of the Spirit is given to every man to profit withal.
>
> **8** For to one is given by the Spirit the word of wisdom; to another the word of knowledge by the same Spirit;
>
> **9** To another faith by the same Spirit; to another the gifts of healing by the same Spirit;
>
> **10** To another the working of miracles; to another prophecy; to another discerning of spirits; to another *divers* kinds of tongues; to another the interpretation of tongues:
>
> **11** But all these worketh that one and the selfsame Spirit, dividing to every man severally as he will.

Consciousness Level #5: Continued development of consciousness by "renewing our minds" to God's values and Word so as to maintain a "spiritual mindset" toward Him.

I Corinthians 2:16(b):

But we have the mind of Christ.

We maintain an ongoing "renewing of the mind" to spiritual truth about God, Christ, Holy Spirit and the reality of our spiritual being. It is a negation of the reality and power of a materialistic world that has no likeness to Spirit.

Romans 12:2:

And be not conformed to this world (matter and materialism) but be ye transformed by the renewing of your mind...

Our spiritual mindset is a mind that is already designed for the purpose of receiving, retaining and releasing the true and accurate Word of God. It accepts truth and exposes errors in thinking. It is comparable to a template for the Word. We are to "lead every thought captive to the Word."

II Cor. 10:5:

...Casting down imaginations and high (false) reasoning that exalts itself against the Word of God and bringing into captivity every thought to the obedience of Christ.

A spiritual mindset is based upon God's love and truth about Him and our eternal relationship with an all knowing, all-powerful, all present God, our Heavenly Father.

PART II
CONSCIOUSNESS OF SPIRITUAL VALUES

5

SPIRITUAL WORSHIP VALUES

Spiritually conscious men and women in Christ can obliterate any opportunity for spiritual oblivion by consistently "renewing their minds" to worship in spirit and truth through a spiritual understanding of the nature of God, His spiritually inspired Word, and a full knowledge and acceptance that we have always had inherent spiritual worthiness.

> Romans 12:2:
> And be not conformed to this world but be ye transformed [changed] by the renewing of your mind, that ye might prove what is that good, and acceptable, and perfect, will of God.

The following spiritual values of God encompass all of true worship:

1. Supremely value ("worship") God, the Father of Jesus Christ

John 4:23-24: But the hour cometh, and now is, when the true worshippers shall worship the Father in spirit and in truth: for the Father seeketh such to worship him. God is a Spirit: and they that worship him must worship him in spirit and in truth.

2. Value Jesus Christ, God's only begotten Son

John 10:10-11: The thief cometh not, but for to steal, and to kill, and to destroy: I am come that they might have life, and that they might have it more abundantly.

John 5:22-23: For the Father judged no man, but hath committed all judgment unto the Son: that all men should honor the Son, even as they honor the Father. He that honored not the Son honored not the Father which hath sent him.

3. Value a spiritual understanding of the accurate Word of God

John 1:1: In the beginning was the Word, and the Word was with God, and the Word was God. The same was in the beginning with God.

II Timothy 2:15: Study to show thyself approved unto God, a workman that needeth not to be ashamed, rightly dividing the word of truth.

II Timothy 3:16-17: All Scripture is given by inspiration of God, and is profitable for doctrine, for reproof, for correction, for instruction in righteousness: that the man of God may be perfect, thoroughly furnished unto all good works.

John 8:31-32: Then said Jesus to those Jews which believed on him, If ye continue in my word, then are ye my disciples indeed; and ye shall know the truth, and the truth shall make you free.

4. Value the work of the "The Comforter" (Holy Spirit)

I Corinthians 2:11-12: For what man knoweth the things of a man, save the spirit of man which is in him? even so the things of God knoweth no man, but the Spirit of God. Now we have received, not the spirit of the world, but the Spirit which is of God; that we might know the things that are freely given to us of God.

John 15:26: But when the Comforter is come, whom I will send unto you from the Father, even the Spirit of truth, which proceedeth from the Father, he shall testify of me:

II Timothy 1:7: For God hath not given us the spirit of fear; but of power, and of love, and of a sound mind.

5. Value "godliness" (an ongoing relationship with God through prayer)

I Timothy 4:8: For bodily exercise profiteth little: but godliness is profitable unto all things, having promise of the life that now is, and of that which is to come.

I Timothy 6:3-7: If any man teach otherwise, and consent not to wholesome words, even the words of our Lord Jesus Christ, and to the doctrine which is according to godliness; he is proud, knowing nothing, but doting about questions and strifes of words, whereof cometh envy, strife, railings, evil surmisings, perverse disputings of men of corrupt minds, and destitute of the truth, supposing that gain is godliness: from such withdraw thyself. But godliness with contentment is great gain. For we brought nothing into this world, and it is certain we can carry nothing out.

6. Value the "One spiritual Body of Christ"

I Corinthians 12:12-13: For as the body is one, and hath many members and all the members of that one body, being many, are one body: so also is Christ. For by one Spirit are we all baptized into one body, whether we be Jews or Gentiles, whether we be bond or free; and have been all made to drink into one Spirit.

7. Value all men for Christ, since we are all "created in God's image (Spirit)"

Genesis 1:26-27: And God said, Let us make man in our image, after our likeness: and let them have dominion over the fish of the sea, and over the fowl of the air, and over the cattle, and over all the earth, and over every creeping thing that creepeth upon the earth. So God created man in his *own* image, in the image of God created he him; male and female created he them.

8. Value man's inherent divine nature and identity

Ephesians 2:10: For we are his workmanship, created in Christ Jesus unto good works, which God hath before ordained that we should walk in them.

II Peter 1:3-4: According as his divine power hath given unto us all things that *pertain* unto life and godliness, through the knowledge of him that hath called us to glory and virtue: whereby are given unto us exceeding great and precious promises; that by these ye might be partakers of the divine nature, having escaped the corruption that is in the world through lust.

9. Value the love of God

Matthew 22:37-39: Jesus said unto him, THOU SHALT LOVE THE LORD THY GOD WITH ALL THY HEART, AND WITH ALL THY SOUL, AND WITH ALL THY MIND This is the first and great [most valued] commandment. And the second is like unto it: thou shalt love thy neighbor as thyself.

Romans 8:38-39: For I am persuaded, that neither death, nor life, nor angels, nor principalities, nor powers, nor things present, nor things to come, nor height, nor depth, nor any other creature, shall be able to separate us from the love of God, which is in Christ Jesus our Lord.

10. Value the wisdom of God

Prov.1: 2-4: To know wisdom and instruction; to perceive the words of understanding; to receive the instruction of wisdom, justice, and judgment, and equity; to give subtilty to the simple, to the young man knowledge and discretion.

Ephesians 1:17-18: That the God of our Lord Jesus Christ, the Father of glory, may give unto you the spirit of wisdom and revelation in the knowledge of him: the eyes of your understanding being enlightened; that ye may know what is the hope of his calling, and what the riches of the glory of his inheritance in the saints.

I Corinthians 1:30-31: But of him are ye in Christ Jesus, who of God is made unto us wisdom, and righteousness, and sanctification, and redemption: that, according as it is written, He that glorieth, let him glory in the Lord.

Synopsis: Spiritual Worship Values of God

Worshipping or supremely valuing God, the Father of Jesus Christ, is the first and main value of God. Toward this goal, we pursue all other spiritual values. We worship or supremely value God, the Father of Jesus Christ, BY valuing His Son, His Word and the Holy Spirit. We value our worth as spiritual beings created in His image, our ongoing relationship with Him ("godliness"), His children ("the One Body of Christ"), His planned return of Christ, and His love and wisdom in Christ.

6

NINE MANIFESTATIONS OF HOLY SPIRIT

For a deeper understanding of true worship and its relationship to *spiritual consciousness* and *spiritual oblivion,* we need to study and appreciate all of the "nine manifestations of Holy Spirit." Our operation of these manifestations will always enhance our spiritual ability to worship God, to receive revelation from Him, and operate the power of the Holy Spirit to carry out His will.

> I Corinthians 12:7-10:
>
> But the manifestation of the Spirit is given to every man to profit [value] withal [immediately and long-term].
>
> For to one [for one's profit and value] is given by the Spirit *the word of wisdom*; to another [for one's profit or value] *the word of knowledge* by the same Spirit;
>
> To another [for one's profit or value] *faith* by the same Spirit; to another [for one's profit or value] the *gifts of healings* by the same Spirit;
>
> To another [for one's profit or value] *the working of miracles*; to another [for one's profit or value] *prophecy*; to another [for one's profit or value] *discerning of spirits*; to another [for one's profit or value] *divers kinds of tongues*; to another [for one's profit or value] *the interpretation of tongues*. .

Word of knowledge, word of wisdom, and *discerning of spirits* provide revelation from God that cannot be attained through the five senses. These three manifestations offer knowledge of a situation (*word of knowledge*), show us what to do about it (*word of wisdom*), and expose spiritually good or evil forces that may be in operation (*discerning of spirits*). Our own thinking or analyzing cannot force this revelation.

Faith, gifts of healings and *the working of miracles* are described as "action manifestations" of the Spirit that provide instant deliverance to others as a result of God's revelation.

The manifestation of *faith* is the spiritual courage to carry out whatever God has revealed to us by word of knowledge, word of wisdom, and/or discerning of spirits.

Speaking in tongues, interpretation of tongues and *prophecy* are considered "worship manifestations" because they involve inspiration and praise to God. Since these are ways to worship God, why wouldn't we want to operate and rigorously pursue them?

Speaking in tongues is speaking in a language unknown to the speaker. To begin to exercise this manifestation, we need to find a quiet location for a period of time, and privately thank God for the God-given capability to speak in tongues. We then simply open our mouths, move our lips and tongue, and allow sounds or words to come forth, as the Spirit gives the utterance (Acts 2:1-4).

Interpretation of tongues is verbally delivering at a believer's meeting the basic essence of what was said in tongues. This message can include words of praise to God or edification and exhortation from God or for God.

Prophecy is speaking for or from God and is always meant to edify, encourage, and comfort the Church. It is bringing forth information concerning God in the language of the people present so that they can easily understand it.

I Corinthians 14:2-5:

For he that speaketh in an unknown tongue speaketh not unto men, but unto God: for no man understandeth him; howbeit in the spirit he speaketh mysteries.

But he that prophesieth speaketh unto men to edification, and exhortation, and comfort.

He that speaketh in an unknown tongue edifieth himself; but he that prophesieth edifieth the church.

I would that ye all spake with tongues, but rather [even more] that ye prophesied: for greater is he that prophesieth than he that speaketh with tongues, except he interpret, that the church may receive edifying.

There are many confused and evil misconceptions concerning the availability and uses of the nine manifestations. People are often fearful of them or lack confidence in God to operate them. They are concerned that the manifestations may be perceived as strange. They believe that these evidences of the Holy Spirit are no longer available or are only for the select few. There errors in thinking lack truth from the Word. We would have to remove the First Book of Corinthians, Chapters 12-14, in order to deny the availability of operating all of the nine manifestations in the true worship of God.

Spiritual consciousness of worship is spiritually understanding and operating all nine manifestations of the Spirit all of the time.

Spiritually conscious worship solutions:

- *Consider the meaning and purpose of each of the nine manifestations.*
- *Research examples, in the Gospels and the Book of Acts, of how believers received revelation from God through word of knowledge, word of wisdom and discerning of spirits.*
- *Pursue examples in Acts to see how believers "worshipped in the Spirit" by speaking in tongues, interpretation of tongues, and prophecy (Acts 8)*
- *Continue to re-read and meditate on scriptures in this chapter*

PART III
SPIRITUAL OBLIVION DEMONSTRATED

True consciousness is the spiritual awareness of our continual need for God's grace in every situation.

Hebrews 4:16:

> Let us therefore come boldly unto the throne of grace, that we may obtain mercy, and find grace to help in time of need.

As the Spirit works in us to pray for inspiration, study the accuracy of the Scriptures and perform other love-based activities, we become more vigilant of spiritual distractions. More frequently than we would like to admit, we may not feel like doing things for God or others. Despite these emotions and attitudes, the Spirit of God will continue to reactivate our spiritual interest in loving and serving.

Devoid of spiritual awareness of his value and worth in God, mortal man lives with persistent sin-consciousness, materialistic thinking, and mental condemnation. Spiritual consciousness of God and the idea that man is created in His spiritual image, are not a part of his mental processes, habit patterns, and decision-making.

As a result of this lack of spiritual sense, man remains spiritually oblivious and lives in a world in which he automatically gravitates toward materialistic mortal values, thoughts and actions that are illusive, false and decadent. He is deceived into thinking that he either has no control because of years of guilt and sin-consciousness or complete control of life because of worldly and prideful errors in thinking.

I John 2:15:

Love not the world, neither the things that are in the world. If any man loves the world, the love of the Father is not in him.

Oblivion continues because of deceptive conflicts between two antagonistic forces, the one true God (who is Spirit and to be worshipped) and the materialistic, natural world ("the flesh").

Both forces are constantly concerned with the lives, hearts, and minds of people.

Both sides want to be loved, worshipped, and served more than anything else.

God, the Father of Jesus Christ, never initiates critical conditions and their consequences. He never sets up a personal, communal or global crisis to make man more spiritual or to test him.

James 1:13-14, 16-17:

Let no man say when he is tempted, I am tempted of God: for God cannot be tempted with evil, neither tempteth He any man:

But every man is tempted, when he is drawn away of his own lust (the five senses; errors in thinking), and enticed.

Do not err, my beloved brethren.

Every good gift and every perfect gift is from above, and cometh down from the Father of lights, with whom is no variableness, neither shadow of turning.

In the absence of true spiritual consciousness, individuals may seek pseudo-spiritual or worldly answers from themselves, others, groups, nature, and even creation more than or instead of God, The One True, Powerful, Knowing, and Loving Creator.

Romans 1:25:

Who changed the truth of God into a lie, and worshipped and served the creature more than the Creator, who is blessed forever. Amen.

7

SPIRITUAL OBLIVION: A DISTORTION OF WORSHIP VALUES

There is a definite relationship between a values, worship and spiritual oblivion. Consistently elevating material or five-sense values above spiritual values and ideas will sustain oblivion. The world (aka "the flesh," materialism, nature, science, matter) and the things of the Spirit are contrary to one another. You cannot mix the two. Perceived human crises are secondary effects of errors in thinking regarding spiritual values.

> John 3:6:
> That which is born of the flesh is flesh; and that which is born of the Spirit is spirit.

> Mathew 6:24:
> No man can serve two masters: for either he will hate the one, and love the other; or else he will hold to the one, and despise the other. Ye cannot serve God and mammon.

In this book, the author defines "spiritual values" as biblically based values directly related to God and spiritual matters of God. These values primarily involve **worship** through prayer, admiration, God's Word, and the worth God has given us. These spiritual values glorify a God who is loving, non-judgmental and does not provide religious laws and rituals. The spiritual values discussed in this chapter DO NOT include religion, nature, humanism or altruism, group involvement, attitudes, love of mankind, or the creation. There is general agreement that the concepts of religion and spirituality are not equivalent and need to be clarified in specific discussions. The author chooses to explore "values" instead of "beliefs" because values allow the individual to pursue greater cognitive and spiritual understanding of God and what He values in His Word, whereas beliefs are assumptions that we think are true but may or may not have a cognitive base.

> *A state of spiritual oblivion is a spiritual crisis or turning point of decision in which we value matter, materialistic thoughts, information and sin-consciousness from the world MORE THAN OR INSTEAD OF spiritual consciousness and ideas from God regarding worship through His Word, and our true inherent spiritual worth.*

If we accept this definition as scripturally accurate, then its opposite must be equally true in defining *spiritual consciousness*, namely:

> *Spiritual consciousness is an ongoing increase in spiritual awareness of true worship values, God's magnified Word, and the spiritual reality that we are "created" in God's image MORE THAN OR INSTEAD OF valuing five-sense, materialistic, worldly thinking, and flawed negativistic habit patterns.*

Galatians 5:17:
> For the flesh lusteth against the Spirit, and the Spirit against the flesh: and these are contrary the one to the other: so that ye cannot do the things that ye would.

What worship values we become conscious of and choose to consistently value will determine the degree of prevailing over or yielding to any perceived crisis in life. When we are spiritually conscious of the true worship of God and His values, have a spiritual understanding concerning His Word, and recognize our divine nature, we will have balance and harmony in our lives.

8

CAUSE AND EFFECT OF MAN'S PROBLEMS

When we consistently lack or lose a sense of spiritual consciousness of God's Divine love and presence, we become increasingly deceived into believing the world's values. Maintaining errors in thinking regarding true worship, true Word and/or our spiritual worth, we become disrupted into believing and acting upon false materialistic values concerning self, others and the world. As a result, *oblivion* continues, whether or not it is manifested or experienced by an individual, community or nation.

In this day and time, all critical human conditions appear to "mortal man" to be primarily a function of internal or external human factors. The world hardly questions, often misunderstands or has no true knowledge that every mortal crisis stems from a lack of spiritual consciousness of God's values and ideas. This state of spiritual oblivion is the cause and effect of all perceived natural critical conditions.

The Bible reveals that the most calamitous crisis, ***spiritual oblivion concerning worship***, originated when Adam lost spiritual consciousness of the truth that he was and always would be a spiritual being, created by God. Adam and Eve not only lost sight of their spiritual identity, but also believed in the power of other unreal, negative forces equal to or greater than God. Finally, Eve did the unthinkable. She added, omitted and ultimately changed God's Word because of serious errors in thinking. These critical thoughts and actions were replaced by a flawed mental sense of sin-consciousness, condemnation and unworthiness (as recorded in Genesis, Chapter Three), which triggered emotional, physical, and systemic catastrophes for all times and for the entire world. Since that time, mortal man replaced spiritual consciousness with sin-consciousness and unrighteousness.

Genesis 3: 1-7 unfolds this major *crisis of spiritual consciousness* with its resulting state of spiritual oblivion:

> Now the serpent was more subtle than any beast of the field which the Lord God had made. And he said unto the woman, Yea, hath God said, Ye shall not eat of every tree of the garden?
>
> And the woman said unto the serpent [She spoke to the serpent who has no vocal chords], We may eat of the fruit of the trees of the garden:
>
> But of the fruit of the tree which is in the midst of the garden, God hath said, Ye shall not eat of it, neither shall ye touch it, lest ye die. [She omitted, added and changed God's Word]
>
> And the serpent said unto the woman, Ye shall not surely die:
>
> For God doth know that in the day ye eat thereof, then your eyes shall be opened, and ye shall be as gods, knowing good and evil.
>
> And when the woman saw that the tree was good for food, and that it was pleasant to the eyes, and a tree to be desired to make one wise, she took of the fruit thereof, and did eat, and gave also unto her husband with her; and he did eat.
>
> And the eyes of them both were opened, and they knew that they were naked; and they sewed fig leaves together, and made themselves aprons [There was a sense of condemnation, sin-consciousness and guilt].

Only God's gracious "crisis intervention" would be able to enlighten man to true spiritual consciousness concerning worship, the Word, and a spiritual sense of true worth. By the word and works of Jesus Christ and "The Comforter" (Holy Spirit), God brought man to heightened levels of reclaiming awareness of truth and love.

> Ephesians 1:17-19:
>
> That the God of our Lord Jesus Christ, the Father of glory, may give unto you the spirit of wisdom and revelation in the knowledge of him:
>
> The eyes of your understanding being enlightened; that ye may know what is the hope of his calling, and what the riches of the glory of his inheritance in the saints,
>
> And what is the exceeding greatness of his power to us-ward who believe, according to the working of his mighty power,

The final step of living in God's *complete spiritual consciousness* will come when Jesus Christ returns and final judgment is completed. Spiritual man will no longer "cry for help" because there will be no more tears or sorrow, but eternal life with God; a life that already has began through Christ.

> John 3:16:
>
> For God so loved the world, that he gave his only begotten Son, that whosoever believeth in him should not perish, but have everlasting life.

In the Book of Revelation, God unfolds a new heaven and new earth for believers in Christ.

Revelation 21:1,3-4:

And I saw a new heaven and a new earth; for the first heaven and the first earth were passed away; and there was no more sea.

And I heard a great voice out of heaven saying, Behold, the tabernacle of God is with men, and He will dwell with them, and they shall be His people, and God Himself shall be with them, and be their God.

And God shall wipe away all tears from their eyes; and there shall be no more death, neither sorrow, nor crying, neither shall there be any more pain: for the former things are passed away.

9

CONVERSION: A SPIRITUAL AWAKENING

God wants all men to be "saved" (made whole) by recognizing their true inherent spiritual identity, which was created in His image and also by an enlightened spiritual knowledge of God and His Son.

> I Timothy 2:4-5:
>> Who [God] will have all men to be saved, and to come unto [by coming to] the knowledge of the truth.
>> For there is one God, and one mediator [one middle man] between God and men, the man Christ Jesus.

God alone is able to command the spiritual consciousness of Christ to shine in our hearts.

> II Corinthians 4:6:
>> For God, who commanded the light to shine out of darkness, hath shined in our hearts, to give the light of the knowledge of the glory of God in the face of Jesus Christ.

When an individual comes to the level of spiritual consciousness of the Word of God concerning Christ, he/she is saved (made whole: *sozo*). He has been delivered from mental condemnation and a deep sense of worthlessness. He has escaped spiritual oblivion and has reclaimed true spiritual consciousness. He is "converted."

The word, "conversion," has several definitions. From *Merriam-Webster's*, it is characterized as, "a definite and decisive adoption of belief." Conversion basically has to do with a change of values or a shift to valuing something or someone else. The word, convert, has its root in **COM + *vertere***, which means, "a turning around to something of greater worth or more value." Often, a "convert" refers to an individual who has turned away from the world and toward another belief. He has been brought from one belief to another of greater worth.

Biblically, conversion occurs when an individual becomes spiritually aware of the divine nature he always had, as recorded in Genesis, Chapter One. Almighty God through His middleman, Jesus Christ, enables this individual to permanently shift to spiritual values.

Through His Son Jesus Christ, He has enlightened man concerning a life "more abundantly."

> John 10:10:
> The thief cometh not, but for to steal, and to kill, and
> to destroy: I am come that they might have life, and that
> they might have it more abundantly.

In Jesus Christ, there is *no crisis*, no turning point; there already is a radical change. God alone has made the decisive difference in resolving all critical issues by spiritually awakening man to a true consciousness of Himself, the Christ spirit in us, and "The Comforter" (Holy Spirit). For those who do not know enough to spiritually understand Jesus Christ or who refuse to open their eyes to look, they remain spiritually blinded and, as a result, the Gospel of Christ cannot be received.

> II Corinthians 4:4:
> In whom the god of this world hath blinded the minds
> of them that believe not lest the light of the glorious gospel

of Christ, who is the image of God, should shine unto them.

> **Jesus Christ stated that there would always be conflict and mental pressure in the material world.**

John 16:33 (b):
> In the world [this material age] ye shall have tribulation [mental pressure; trouble; conflicts because you live in and are distracted by the values of the world]: but be of good cheer; I have overcome the world.

There is "good cheer" or "well-balanced thinking" in accepting the conscious spiritual reality of Jesus Christ and Christ the resurrected One as the answer to conflicts for all. To quote an outstanding preacher that I have known for many decades: *"You tell me what you think of Jesus Christ, and I'll tell you how far you will go spiritually."*

The Apostle Paul reminded believers in Christ that there will be continued pressure from the world because of their stand for God.

II Timothy 2:12:
> Yea, and all that will live godly in Christ Jesus shall suffer persecution.

When spiritual man practices the constant presence of God and attempts to live in accordance with His Word, he will have deceptive assaults from the world.

> **Every worldly so-called "crisis" that mortal man faces today is the cause and/or effect of spiritual oblivion of**

worship of God's presence, power, truth, Word, and love.

An ongoing *spiritual oblivion* is the result of being spiritually clueless to the world's distorted maneuvers. We are unaware of the truth concerning real spiritual worship of God and the reality of His Son, Jesus Christ. The material world tries to place endless evil suggestions in our minds so that we do not want to, or cannot understand the Word or believe the promises of God. We remain utterly confused about who we are spiritually and how and what to worship.

Day by day, spiritual man needs to remain vigilant of negative worldly forces that constantly attempt to bring strife and disharmony into his life and into the lives of the people he loves. The world entices us to worship others and ourselves, and not to trust in God.

> Proverbs 3:5-6:
> Trust in the Lord with all thine heart; and lean not unto thine own understanding.
> In all thy ways, acknowledge him and he shall direct they path.

> II Peter 5:8-9:
> Be sober [keep your thoughts well-arranged with the Scriptures], be vigilant; because your adversary the devil, as a roaring lion seeketh whom he may devour:
> Whom resist stedfast in the faith, knowing that the same afflictions are accomplished in your brethren that are in the world.

Solutions to Return to Spiritual Consciousness:

Spiritual consciousness of God and Christ is a journey of "spiritual refocus". It is a "spiritual mindset" that involves four biblically based actions:

1) *Attend to God*
   Proverbs 5:1-2: My son, attend unto my wisdom, and bow thine ear to my understanding:

   That thou mayest regard discretion, and thy lips may keep knowledge.

2) *Take heed to His Word to the point of action*
   I Timothy 4:16: Take heed unto thyself, and unto the doctrine; continue in them: for in so doing this thou shalt both save thyself, and them that hear thee.

3) *Pray and watch for the results of His intervention*
   Ephesians 6:18: Praying always with all prayer and supplication [specific requests] in the Spirit, and watching thereunto with all perseverance and supplication for all the saints.

4) *Ask God for increased spiritual awareness*
   Ephesians 1:18-20:
   The eyes of your understanding being enlightened; that ye may know what is the hope of his calling, and what the riches of the glory of his inheritance in the saints,

   And what is the exceeding greatness of his power to us-ward who believe, according to the working of his mighty power,

   Which he wrought in Christ, when he raised him from the dead, and set him at his own right hand in the heavenly places...

10

SPIRITUAL MAN'S RETURN TO OBLIVION

Spiritual man endeavors to live for God through a spiritual understanding of His Word. Daily, he mentally puts on the "armor of God" by studying the Word of God and by prayer. It is because he is standing on the Word of God that worldly fears and beliefs concerning so-called natural crises cannot overturn or influence his thought patterns and solutions. He has done nothing wrong to cause a natural crisis. The world with its false information tries to impose supposed crises upon him *because he is doing something right*. As a result of worldly indirect maneuvers by way of circumstances and people, he is continually faced with false perceptions of natural crisis.

When he allows fear or some other more intense emotion to take over because of shifts away from spiritual to material conditions, he begins to break fellowship with God. Now, he is faced with issues of unbelief, mistrust and distorted worship of God. He needs to be in a spiritual situation with other believers who can and must remind him of his worth in God. However, he may be blinded into refusing the help of others. He needs more instruction regarding his righteousness in the sight of God. But he has become distracted by his current material condition and may stop reading the Word of God. Although he needs to be reminded of his completeness in Christ, he tricks himself out of seeking the community of believers to help him to be strengthened to trust God.

Surrounded by other carnal individuals who foster fear or worldly responses to natural crises, he finds that his mind is systematically open to outside negative influences. He responds to circumstances in an ungodly fashion by seeking out answers from the world more than from God. Without realizing it, a spiritual fear, a lack of valor, or some other traumatizing emotion has allowed him to shift his values away from Christ and toward the wisdom of the world. His mental understanding and conviction of his spiritual worth and righteousness in Christ are shaken. He falls into spiritual oblivion guided by sin-consciousness and begins to look at natural reasons for and immediate solutions to his crisis. This spiritual man now has moved into full-blown spiritual oblivion. He ignores the inner prompting of the Holy Spirit and forgets to ask God for help so as to return to correct ways of thinking concerning spiritual values. If he ignores or refuses to follow the Spirit of God, he will continue to make choices that are ungodly, unwise, and out of balance with the Word of God. This spiritual man is now thinking and acting as a natural, mortal man.

His thoughts and words are consumed by worldly approaches to handling problems. He may continue to feel that he is "spiritual," but his actions and words say otherwise. When he has found answers that seem reasonable, he may even endeavor to become "preachy" and legalistic regarding worldly ways to handle crises. As he continues to turn his heart and values in the direction of the world, his natural crisis seems more real than perceived, and his spiritual oblivion escalates. In these situations, a Word-based counselor, informally or formally, can help to discern the individual's chronic errors in thinking about God, worship, the Word, and/or his worthiness.

The true spiritual man knows his "son-ship" rights with God and endeavors to keep fellowship with Him. He surrounds himself with others who remind him of his righteousness and the power, love and goodness of God. He is spiritually conscious of the systems of the world and their devices. He often seeks feedback from other spiritually conscious individuals regarding his false thinking and how it impacts on his perceived natural crisis. He keeps his eye on the hope of the return of Christ knowing that, if all else fails, he has eternal life *now*. In truth, spiritual man knows and accepts that a so-called "natural crisis" is unreality, is assured that he is complete in Christ, and has a divine nature. For him, God has already handled sickness, fear and death.

For spiritual man who continues to trust God, natural crises are not real or acceptable. This individual rigorously pursues personal ongoing intervention with God through continued study of the Scriptures concerning Christ, the values of God, and his own spiritual valueness. He knows the importance of fellowshipping with spiritually minded believers. He seeks spiritual understanding from God regarding spiritual causes and effects. He knows the role of people, places and things that can torment and distract from right thinking.

11

WORSHIP OBLIVION

The Scriptures present the tragedy of man's spiritual unawareness and disrupted sense of values regarding worship and service.

Romans 1:25:

Who changed the truth of God into a [THE] lie [an error in thinking], and worshipped [supremely valued] and served the creature [self, others, the world] more than [worshipping and serving] the Creator [God], who is blessed forever. Amen.

In this verse, the word, worshipped, comes from the Greek word, *sebazo*, which means, "to reverence," "venerate," "honor," "exalt," "hold in awe," and "to value supremely" (*Young's Analytical Concordance*). Reference here is to a personal respect, appreciation, and awe for God.

"The truth" in Romans 1:25 is that God Almighty is to be supremely valued or worshipped instead of and more than anything else. God is all knowing, all-powerful and all loving.

Exodus 20: 1-4:

And God spake all these words, saying,

I am the Lord thy God, which have brought thee out of the land of Egypt, out of the house of bondage.

Thou shalt have no other gods before me.

Thou shalt not make unto thee any graven image, or any likeness of any thing that is in heaven above, or that is in the earth beneath, or that is in the water under the earth.

For the spiritual man who is consciously open to God, worship (*sebomai*) takes on a deeper spiritual meaning involving an ongoing spiritual relationship with God as *Abba*, Father. This personal communication is only available to one who understands God spiritually.

Romans 8:14-15:
For as many as are led by the Spirit of God, they are the sons of God.

For ye have not received the Spirit of bondage again to fear; but ye have received the Spirit of adoption, whereby we cry, *Abba*, Father.

Galatians 4:6:
And because ye are sons, God hath sent forth the Spirit of his Son into your hearts, crying *Abba*, Father.

A heightened level of consciousness of worship became intensified for man because of the accomplished work of Christ and the coming of "The Comforter" (Holy Spirit) at Pentecost. Since then, spiritual man recognizes that he has direct spiritual access to God.

Ephesians 2:18:
For through him [Jesus Christ] we have access by one Spirit unto the Father.

In the Epistle to the Philippians 3:3, the Apostle Paul stated:

For we are the circumcision [of the heart], which worship God in the Spirit, and rejoice in Christ Jesus, and have no confidence in the flesh.

We worship God in spirit BY rejoicing in Christ Jesus, the resurrected one, and giving no power or value to materiality and mortal man thinking.

John4: 24:
God is spirit, and they that worship Him must worship Him in spirit and in truth.

When we worship Him materially or externally and when we choose to keep errors in thinking instead of accepting truth, we are not worshipping God spiritually or truthfully.

When we are mentally deceived into valuing anything above God and the things of God, we are operating by old ways of worldly thinking instead of acting by the divine nature of the Christ within us.

In worship oblivion, the deception behind all deceptions is the spiritual blindness and false thinking that someone or something is to be valued MORE THAN OR INSTEAD OF God in Christ.

We will reclaim spiritual worship consciousness by growing in the spiritual consciousness of God in Christ as greatly valued MORE THAN OR INSTEAD OF five-sense thinking of oneself, other people, material things, nature, and/or creation.

When we value something instead of or more than God, we are valuing and being dominated by the world's systems and erroneous ideals. We have allowed false ideas and mistaken mental habit patterns of self and the world to outweigh spiritually conscious ideas, words, and actions of the heart. This is the worship of idols. We can "flee from idolatry" by putting God first and foremost above all else.

I Corinthians 10:13-14:

There hath no temptation taken you but such as is common to man: but God is faithful, who will not suffer [allow] you to be tempted above that ye are able; but will with the temptation also make a way to escape, that ye may be able to bear it.

Wherefore, my beloved brethren, flee from idolatry (spiritual oblivion, nothingness, delusion).

In the Book of I Kings, when Elijah assembled the false prophets in Mount Carmel, he went before the people and questioned their shift in thinking and values.

I Kings 18: 21:

How long will you waver [sink; become lame] between two opinions [values]? If the Lord is God, follow him: but if Baal [which means lord or spiritual master], then follow him.

By revelation from God, Joshua presented a similar issue regarding worship and service to the tribes of Israel gathered in Shechem.

Joshua 24:14-15:

Now therefore fear the Lord, and serve him in sincerity and truth: and put away the gods which your fathers served on the other side of the flood, and in Egypt; and serve ye the Lord.

And if it seem evil unto you to serve the Lord, choose you this day whom ye will serve; whether the gods which your fathers served that were on the other side of the flood, or the gods of the Amerites, in whose land ye dwell: but as for me and my house, we will serve the Lord.

In his Sermon on the Mount, Jesus pointed out the need to serve God above all else. We cannot maintain a spiritual balance between God and the material world. God is real. The material world is unreal.

Matthew 5:24:

No man can serve [*douleuo*] two masters: for either he will hate the one, and love the other; or else he will hold to the one, and despise the other. You cannot serve God and mammon [matter, the world].

PART IV
SPIRITUAL DIMENSIONS OF
WORSHIP OBLIVION

Falsely worshipping or not supremely valuing God, the Father of Jesus Christ, is the first and main oblivion. Because of a lack of spiritual consciousness of God, we cannot truthfully pursue all other spiritual values. We remain oblivious to worship or supremely value God, the Father of Jesus Christ, BY unconsciously devaluing His Son, His Word and the Holy Spirit. We fail to recognize our worth as spiritual beings created in His image, our ongoing relationship with Him ("godliness"), His children ("the One Body of Christ"), His planned return of Christ, and His love and wisdom in Christ.

Worship oblivion has several dimensions that can be understood more clearly by categorizing these dimensions into three parts:

1. *Oblivion of Worship of an all loving and powerful Father*
2. *Oblivion of the Word of God*
3. *Oblivion of Spiritual Worth*

12

OB #1: LOVE OBLIVION

Love oblivion *is consistently giving value to the fake and deceitful love of oneself, others, and/or the world MORE THAN OR INSTEAD OF the unconditional true love of and from God through Christ. The outcome of this oblivion is false worship, and distorted or elevated relationships filled with disappointment and accusations.*

Reclaim love consciousness *by consistently giving value to the unconditional true love of and from God through Christ MORE THAN OR INSTEAD OF the hypocritically fake and deceitful love of oneself, others, and/or the world.*

People continue to express confusion regarding how to give, receive, and sustain love. Few acknowledge that the real critical condition of love is spiritual. Love oblivion involves a deceptive search for love from sources other than the one true God.

I John 4:8, 16(b):

He that loveth not knoweth not God; for God is love....

God is love; and he that dwelleth in love dwelleth in God and God in him.

Ongoing personal problems and chaotic interpersonal relationships are directly related to spiritual unawareness of giving to and receiving love from God. The ability to love starts with God through His Son, Jesus Christ.

> I John 4:19:
>> We love, because he first loved us.

> John 3:16:
>> For God so loved the world that he gave his only begotten Son, that whosoever believeth in him should not perish, but have everlasting life.

God made us acceptable and gave us the ability to receive His love.

> Romans 5:8:
>> But God commended his love toward us [presented us worthy of acceptance of love], in that, while we were yet sinners [with errors in thought and action], Christ died for us.

The Scriptures remind us that we are to love God first and then love our neighbor as ourselves. The only way we can love others and ourselves is to stay "head over heels" in love with God.

> Matthew 22: 37-39:
>> Jesus said unto him, THOU SHALT LOVE THE LORD THY GOD WITH ALL THY HEART, AND WITH ALL THY SOUL, AND WITH ALL THY MIND. This is the first and great [most valued] commandment. And the second is like unto it, THOU SHALT LOVE THY NEIGHBOR AS THYSELF.

No amount of help or guidance centered on self-love or love of others will ever free us from love oblivion. To be delivered, we need to refocus on God and His love.

> Romans 12:9:
> Let love [*agape*] be without dissimulation [*hupocrisis*]. Abhor that which is evil; cleave to that which is good.

> Matthew 6:16:
> When you fast, be not, as the hypocrites, of a sad countenance: for they disfigure their faces, that they may appear unto men to fast. Verily I say unto you, They have their reward.

The Scriptures discourage us from being phony or hypocritical in love. Instead, we are encouraged to synchronize our hearts, words, and actions with God's love. We do not feel one way and act another. We are not to wear masks to cover up the loving person God made us to be in Christ. To "love without dissimulation" or hypocrisy, we allow ourselves to love with truthfulness (of Spirit and Word). We abhor evil, not by legalistically trying to stop evil (flawed thinking/action). We abhor it by cleaving to "that which is good." Good is right thinking and action from the Word. Love without hypocrisy is putting greater weight and value on what is good, namely, God and His Word. As a result, we will put less weight on negative thinking and ultimately "abhor evil."

> *As spiritual beings created in His image, we are to be very loving with one another and without ulterior motives.*

Romans 12:10:

Be kindly affectioned one to another with brotherly love; in honour preferring one another.

Often, mortal man misconstrues the manifestations of the love of God by spiritually love conscious individuals. He/she distorts sincere displays of God's love and may see them as sexual or evil. This is fear on his/her part. These misperceptions are seeds of a **love oblivion** because of the person's previous history of distorted worldly love, such as dysfunctional family patterns, rejected lovers, domestic violence, sexual abuse, and/or a lack of knowledge of the Word of God concerning spiritually-based love.

We are always in the business of love. By demonstrating the love of God toward others, we continue to shift our values toward Christ and heightened spiritual awareness. We have the capacity to overcome errors in thought and resulting behaviors by saturating ourselves with Word-based ideas and loving actions.

True spiritual love of/from God energizes our believing.

Galatians 5:6:

For in Jesus Christ neither circumcision [self-works] availeth [is profitable or valuable for] any thing nor uncircumcision; but faith which worketh [is energized] by love [the love of God].

Phony, pretended, or withheld love builds confusion and fear.

I John 4:18:

There is no fear in love; but perfect love casteth out fear: because fear hath torment [punishment]. He that feareth is not made perfect in love.

When the genuine love of God is in our minds and manifested, it stems from a humble heart that values the Word of God, desires good habit patterns, and honestly believes in God's unconditional love for us, His children.

> I Timothy 1:5:
>> Now the end [goal] of the commandment is charity [the love of God manifested] out of a pure heart, and of good conscience, and of faith unfeigned.

God, His Son Jesus Christ, and the Holy Spirit help us to harmonize our hearts and attitudes with genuine spiritual love. God can show us the truth of His love through Christ's compassion and the love of the Spirit. He can reveal *how* to love others in ways that truly meet their needs. The genuine love of God in evidence never fails to overcome any situation. Spiritual man already has the love of God spiritually from the time he was created in His image, but he may never manifest it. He maintains the *oblivion of love* because his mind or heart is chronically out of balance with God's Word and will. His thoughts, words, and actions are out of harmony with his spiritual capacity to love.

13

SPIRITUALLY CONSCIOUS LOVE

Varied characteristics of the love of God in one's mind and in evidence are provided in I Corinthians, Chapter 13.

Verse 4:
Charity suffereth long, and is kind; charity envieth not; charity vaunteth not itself, is not puffed up.

The love of God in our renewed mind is patient and kind. It does not show jealousy or envy. It does not brag or think it is better than someone else. A shift toward *love oblivion* can develop, as we consistently manifest the worldly opposites of God's love, such as pretended love, impatience, jealousy, pride, and/or selfish self-importance.

Verse 5:
[Charity] Doth not behave itself unseemly, seeketh not her own, is not easily provoked, thinketh no evil.

The love of God toward oneself or others is not out of order or disruptive. It is not selfish and does not lose emotional control.

Verses 6-7:
[Charity] Rejoiceth not in iniquity, but rejoiceth in the truth;
Beareth all things, believeth all things, hopeth all things, endureth all things.

God's love in manifestation does not enjoy or relish in the weaknesses of others. Instead, it is interested in bearing others' burdens and maintaining hope under stressful conditions.

Love oblivion continues to be manifested as the various spiritual characteristics of love become consistently distorted in the direction of worldly views of love. God's specific prayer for us is to be rooted and grounded in His love and to know the love of Christ.

> Ephesians 3:17-19:
> That Christ may dwell in your hearts by faith; that ye, being rooted and grounded in love,
> May be able to comprehend with all the saints [spiritual men and women] what is the breadth, and length, and depth, and height [of that love];
> And to know the love of Christ, which passeth knowledge, that we might be filled with all the fulness of God.

We may make seemingly right judgments based upon the Word of God; however, these decisions often lack love and mercy. God wants us to show love, the love of God and His love for us, even when someone deserves punishment. Consistently thinking evil (maintaining errors in mental patterns) or judging others without mercy leaves us at risk for oblivion. Jesus stressed the importance of forgiveness and mercy in making judgments about others. In Matthew, Chapter 18, he discussed the decision of a certain king who wanted to assess the work of his servants.

> Verses 24-25:
> And when he [the king] had begun to reckon, one was brought unto him, which owed him ten thousand talents [$52,800,000 worth of silver].

But forasmuch as he had not to pay, his lord commanded him to be sold, and his wife, and children, and all that he had, and payment to be made.

Did the king have the legal right to do this? Absolutely. It was the correct decision according to the law. Did the servant deserve punishment? Anyone logically would agree, but watch what transpires. Look at the king's final judgment when compassion, mercy, and forgiveness are involved.

Verses 26-27:

The servant therefore fell down, and worshipped him, saying, Lord, have patience with me, and I will pay thee all.

Then the lord of that servant was moved with compassion, and loosed him, and forgave him the debt.

What a change of heart! Judgment was tempered with mercy in this scenario. Jesus shows us what happens when we do not show mercy and forgiveness toward someone who deserves punishment.

Verses 28-34:

But the same servant went out, and found one of his fellow servants, which owed him a hundred pence ($44): and he laid hands on him and took him by the throat, saying, Pay me that [what] thou owest.

And his fellow servant fell down at his feet, and besought him, saying, Have patience with me, and I will pay thee all.

And he would not: but went and cast him into prison, till he should pay the debt.

So when his fellow servants saw what was done, they were very sorry, and came and told unto their lord all that was done.

Then his lord, after he had called him, said unto him, O thou wicked servant, I forgave thee all that debt, because thou desirest me.

Shouldest not thou also have compassion [mercy] on thy fellow servant, even as I had pity on thee?

And his lord was wroth, and delivered him to the tormentors, till he pay all that was due unto him.

As God in Christ forgave us when we deserved punishment, we are also to temper any judgment of others with mercy and compassion. If we do otherwise, we will "torment" ourselves by this unmerciful decision.

> *Reclaim love consciousness. Consistently give value to the unconditional true love of and from God through Christ MORE THAN OR INSTEAD OF the hypocritically fake and deceitful love of oneself, others, and/or the world*

Spiritually conscious love strategies:

- ➤ Love of God first
- ➤ Love God above all else
- ➤ Love ourselves the way God loves us
- ➤ Love of God in evidence includes affection, service, patience, comfort and forgiveness
- ➤ Love of God is being likeminded on the Word concerning Christ Jesus
- ➤ Love of God does not judge or speak negatively of others

> ➤ Love of God bears others' burdens by exhorting, warning, and submitting to one another
> ➤ Study and meditate on the scriptures in this chapter to gain further spiritual understanding of love
> ➤ Pursue a word study on *agape* love using a Bible concordance

14

OB #2: NEED/SUFFICIENCY OBLIVION

<u>Need/sufficiency oblivion</u> is consistently giving value to self-sufficiency, pride and materialism MORE THAN OR INSTEAD OF valuing God's sufficiency and our completeness in Christ. This oblivion can be manifested by over-achievement, over-concern with stocks, savings, retirement funding, the hoarding of objects, pressure to succeed, and irrational striving for status.

<u>Reclaim spiritually conscious need/sufficiency:</u> Consistently value God's sufficiency and man's completeness in Christ MORE THAN OR INSTEAD OF self-sufficiency and the material things of this world.

Biblical research of the phrase, "err from the faith," provides deeper spiritual insight into the ***oblivion of need/sufficiency.***

I Timothy 6:9-10:

And they that will be rich fall into temptation and a snare [trap], and into many foolish and hurtful lusts, which drown men in destruction and perdition.

For the love of money is the root of all evil [incorrect thinking and actions]: which while some coveted after, they have erred from [concerning] the faith [have mistakenly forgotten or refused to believe their spiritual nature and the accomplished work of Christ], and pierced themselves through with many sorrows.

In this *need/sufficiency oblivion,* the major error in thinking is outweighing God's sufficiency with the love of materialism. We are to put our total trust in God. He is our complete sufficiency and is enough for us in all situations of life. He fills and fulfills all aspects of our lives. He is our all and all. He is enough for us in every way.

Proverbs 3:5-6:
Trust in the Lord with all thine heart; and lean not unto thine own understanding.
In all thy ways acknowledge Him, and He shall direct thy paths.

Psalm 37:3-5 beautifully expresses the totality of His sufficiency:
Trust in the Lord, and do good [Trusting in the Lord IS doing good!]; so shalt thou dwell in the land, and verily thou shalt be fed.
Delight thyself also in the Lord; and He shall give thee the desires of thine heart [God will actually place new desires in your heart, which are in line with His spiritual qualities, our divine nature, and Word.].
Commit thy way unto the Lord; trust also in him; and he shall bring it to pass.

Our sufficiency in God is through our spiritual consciousness of Christ Jesus.

II Corinthians 3:4-5:

> And such trust have we through Christ to God-ward;
>
> Not that we are sufficient of ourselves to think anything as of ourselves; but our sufficiency is of God.

The oblivion of need/sufficiency is maintained when we live consistently for ourselves without realizing that we have God's grace and sufficiency in all things. This *lack of spiritual awareness* is also maintained when we choose to remain isolated from other spiritually conscious believers. Because God supplies all of our needs through Christ Jesus, He wants us to be "cheerful givers" who can thankfully give of our abundance on all levels of service to the spiritual body of believers.

II Corinthians 9:6-8:

> But this I say, He which soweth sparingly shall reap also sparingly; and he which soweth bountifully shall reap also bountifully.
>
> Every man according as he purposeth in his heart, so let him give; not grudgingly, or of necessity: for God loveth a cheerful giver.
>
> And God is able to make all grace abound toward you; that ye, always having all sufficiency in all things, may abound to every good work.

We are cheerful givers BECAUSE God is our sufficiency. We do not give in order to gain His sufficiency, since we already have it in Christ.

Through a greater spiritual understanding of Christ, there is true consciousness of our sufficiency in God. The Scriptures remind us that we are completely complete in Christ.

Colossians 2:8-10:

Beware lest any man spoil you through philosophy and vain deceit, after the tradition of men, after the rudiments [principles] of the world, and not after Christ.

For in him dwelleth all the fulness of the Godhead bodily.

And ye are complete [completely, completely, absolutely complete] in him, which is the head of all principality and power.

The Apostle Paul stressed the importance of valuing godliness (our ongoing personal fellowship with God) more than worldly things.

I Timothy 6:6-11:

But godliness with contentment is great gain [very valuable].

For we brought nothing into the world, and it is certain we can carry nothing out.

And having food and raiment [clothing] let us be therewith content [satisfied].

And they that will be rich fall into temptation and a snare, and into many foolish and hurtful lusts, which drown men in destruction and perdition.

For the love of money is the root of all evil [negativity]: which while some coveted after, they have erred from the faith [They have hurt their ongoing relationship with God by deceptions and unbelief in the Word of Christ], and pierced themselves through with many sorrows.

But thou, O man of God, flee these things; and follow after righteousness, godliness, faith, love, patience, meekness.

Jesus told the story of a man who coveted material possessions instead of being content with God and His sufficiency.

Luke 12:15-21:

And he said unto them, Take heed, and beware of covetousness [wanting more]: for a man's life consisteth not in the abundance of the things which he possesseth.

And he spake a parable unto them saying, The ground of a certain rich man brought forth plentifully:

And he thought within himself, saying, What shall I do, because I have no room where to bestow my fruits?

And he said, This will I do: I will pull down my barns and build greater, and there will I bestow all my fruit and my goods.

And I will say to my soul, Soul, thou hast much goods laid up for many years; take thine ease, eat, drink, and be merry.

But God said unto him, Thou fool, this night shall thy soul be required of thee: then whose shall those things be, which thou hast provided? So is he that layeth up treasures for himself, and is not rich toward God.

Jesus knew the spiritual principle of sufficiency.

Luke 12:29-34:

And seek not ye what ye shall eat, or what ye shall drink, neither be ye of doubtful mind.

For all these things do the nations of the world seek after: and your Father knoweth that ye have need of these things.

But rather seek ye the kingdom of God; and all these things shall be added unto you.

Fear not, little flock; for it is your Father's good pleasure to give you the kingdom. Sell that ye have, and give alms; provide yourselves bags which wax not old, a treasure in the heavens that faileth not, where no thief approacheth, neither moth corrupt.

For where your treasure is [what you value], there will your heart be also.

We have found the treasure we have been looking for all of our lives, which is God in Christ in us, "the hope of [the] glory" (Colossians 1:27).

> *Proclaim and reclaim spiritual consciousness of need-sufficiency: Consistently value God's sufficiency and spiritual man's completeness in Christ MORE THAN OR INSTEAD OF self-sufficiency and the material things of this world.*

Reclaim need/sufficiency consciousness by the following strategies:

➤ Thank God for being our total sufficiency in all things
➤ Be convinced that only God already has supplied all of our need in Christ Jesus
➤ Thank God by service to others
➤ Remember the grace of His sufficiency by abundantly sharing our finances with a church or group that has similar beliefs as ours
➤ Rigorously desire to move the Word of God and His spiritual truth and love
➤ Accept the truth that God is all knowing, all-powerful, and ever present
➤ Continue to re-read and meditate on the scriptures in this chapter

15

OB #3: DISCERNING OBLIVION

The oblivion of discerning is chronically evaluating situations by the five senses, theories and vain philosophies MORE THAN OR INSTEAD OF seeking spiritual inspiration and revelation from God.

Spiritually conscious discerning: Seek inspiration and revelation from God through prayer, the Word and consciousness of His love MORE THAN OR INSTEAD OF chronically evaluating situations by the five senses, theories and vain philosophy.

In addition to the Scriptures, one of the significant ways that God works in us is by way of the Holy Spirit.

> Philippians 2:13:
> For it is God which [who] worketh in you both to will and to do of His good pleasure.

As spiritual beings, we have the ability to operate *the nine manifestations of the Spirit.*

> Corinthians 12:7-10:
> But the manifestation of the Spirit is given to every man to profit [value] withal [immediately and long-term].

For to one [for one's profit and value] is given by the Spirit *the word of wisdom*; to another [for one's profit or value] *the word of knowledge* by the same Spirit;

To another [for one's profit or value] *faith* by the same Spirit; to another [for one's profit or value] the *gifts of healings* by the same Spirit;

To another [for one's profit or value] *the working of miracles*; to another [for one's profit or value] *prophecy*; to another [for one's profit or value] DISCERNING OF SPIRITS [**diakrisis**]; to another [for one's profit or value] *divers kinds of tongues*; to another [for one's profit or value] *the interpretation of tongues*.

The Greek word, **diakrisis**, comes from its root word, **crisis**, which means "discerning." The manifestation *of discerning of spirits* is God's revealing to us, by way of the Holy Spirit, what spiritually good or flawed ideas or actions are operating in different situations. By way of this manifestation, God can reveal to us spiritual causes and effects, and the powers and principalities (mortal errors in principles and thinking) behind them.

Ephesians 6:12:

For we wrestle not against flesh and blood (mortal man), but against principalities, against powers, against the rulers of the darkness of this world, against spiritual wickedness in high places (spiritual oblivion of the power and presence of God).

There are indirect and perceived materialistic and negative forces that subtly affect us by "pushing our buttons" emotionally and by getting us to err in our thinking instead of renewing our thoughts to the Word of God.

These indirect influences work through people, places, and things to block or affect our believing in God. By His grace and choice, God can unveil to us whether or not there is a direct or indirect spiritual influence involved, exactly what specific errors are at work, what these forces are attempting to do, and how to handle them.

In the Four Gospels, there are many examples of Jesus operating the manifestation of discerning of spirits in order to spiritually handle an individual's physical, mental, and emotional conditions.

> Mark 1:34:
> And he [Jesus] healed many that were sick of divers [various] diseases, and cast out many devils; and suffered [allowed] not the devils to speak, because they knew him.

Mark 1:23-26 tells of a man who was incapacitated because of devil spirits (or errors in thinking about sickness):

> And there was in the synagogue a man with an unclean spirit; and he cried out,
> Saying, Let us alone; what have we to do with thee, thou Jesus of Nazareth? Art thou come to destroy us? I know thee who thou art, the Holy One of God.
> And Jesus rebuked him, saying Hold thy peace, and come out of him.
> And when the unclean spirit had torn him, and cried with a loud voice, he came out of him.

Would you say that this was a crisis for the man? As a result of his operating the three manifestations of discerning of spirits, gifts of healings, and the workings of miracles, Jesus healed the man immediately.

Mark 1:27:

And they [the people observing] were all amazed, insomuch that they questioned among themselves, saying, What thing is this? What new doctrine is this? For with authority commandeth he [Jesus] even the unclean [devil] spirits, and they do obey him.

In Mark, Chapter 5, Jesus helped a man from out of the tombs who had many spirits. He discerned by revelation that significant errors in thinking were operating in the man, and asked the spirits directly to identify themselves. Jesus then rebuked them from the man and, miraculously, he was healed of his spiritual and mental crises.

Verse 15:

And they [the people] come to Jesus, and see him that was possessed with the devil, and had the legion, sitting, and clothed, and in his right mind; and they were afraid.

How compassionately Jesus healed the man by spiritually getting rid of the mental and spiritual forces that were blocking and tormenting his thoughts, ideas and overall quality of life.

Verses 18-20:

And when he [Jesus] was come into the ship, he that had been possessed with the devil prayed him that he [the man] might be with him [Jesus].

Howbeit Jesus suffered [allowed] him not, but saith unto him, Go home to thy friends, and tell them how great things the Lord hath done for thee, and hath had compassion on thee.

And he [the man] departed, and began to publish in Decapolis how great things Jesus had done for him: and all men did marvel.

The man was encouraged to handle his deliverance by proclaiming his healing wholeness to all of his friends.

16

BOOK OF ACTS AND DISCERNING OF SPIRITS

There are many examples in the Book of Acts that demonstrate how spiritual men and women handled devil spirits (significant and negative errors in thinking and living).

> Acts 16:16-18:
>
> And it came to pass, as we went to prayer, a certain damsel possessed with the Spirit of divination [spirit of soothsaying] met us, which brought her masters much gain by soothsaying [fortune telling]:
>
> The same followed Paul and us, and cried saying, These men are the servants of the most high God, which shew unto us the way of salvation. And this did she many days.
>
> But Paul, being grieved [irritated spiritually], turned and said to the Spirit, I command thee in the name of Jesus Christ to come out of her. And he came out the same hour.

Paul's discerning of spirits helped him to minister effectively to this woman who was ensnared by a loss of free will. Devil spirits (pervasive and distorted errors in thinking) kept her in spiritual bondage.

> II Timothy 2:26:
>
> And that they may recover themselves out of the snare [trap; crisis] of the devil, who is taken captive by him at his will.

The Greek word, **krino** (related to **crisis**) and its variations further our understanding of discerning. For example, **anakrino** means, "not to examine or ask a question but to spiritually discern." It entails a discerning that is not to be examined by the mind. Without the Spirit of God in operation, natural five-senses man cannot spiritually discern or comprehend situations and crises. He is in spiritual oblivion.

> I Corinthians 2:14:
> But the natural man receiveth not the things of the
> Spirit of God: for they are foolishness unto him: neither
> can he know them, because they are spiritually discerned
> [**anakrino**].

The manifestation of discerning of spirits is not subject to intellectual analyses. Through a continued bombardment of the Word of God, spiritual man endeavors to have his mind attuned to think about spiritual matters and to seek spiritual solutions to all critical conditions.

> Hebrews 5:14:
> But strong meat [deeper understanding of the Word
> of God] belongeth to them that are of full age [mature],
> even those who by reason of use have their senses exercised
> [trained] to discern [**anakrino**] good and evil.

In ministering to others, we need to carry out what God tells us to do regarding discerning of spirits in tormented individuals who have allowed negative thought patterns to infiltrate their lives and wills and maintain oblivion.

> II Timothy 2:24-26:
> And the servant of the Lord must not strive [be in
> strife]; but be gentle unto all men, apt to teach, patient,

In meekness instructing those that oppose themselves [put pressure on themselves; are overbalanced toward self and worldly values]; if God peradventure [at some time] will give them repentance [a change or shift] to the acknowledging of the truth;

And that they may recover themselves [come to their right senses] out of the snare [trap; crisis] of the devil, who are taken captive by him at his will.

Since God has made available to us the nine manifestations of the Spirit (I Corinthians 12:7-11), it would be a serious kink in our spiritual armor not to know or to deny the existence of them. By ignoring, not wanting to know, or refusing to operate discerning of spirits, we will be deceived regarding the spiritual truth behind physical situations and may end up blaming ourselves, people, and/or circumstances. We continue in a state of spiritual oblivion. Projecting blame onto others for how we are being treated instead of realizing the spiritual nature of the problem adds to our present difficult situation. As a result, we can build unwanted bitterness or inner turmoil.

Hebrews 12:15:

Looking diligently [watching carefully] lest any man fail of the grace of God; lest any root of bitterness springing up trouble [inoculate] you, and thereby many be defiled.

If we chronically value decisions based upon five senses thinking more than spiritual insight and understanding, the *oblivion of discerning* will continue. There are some people, in and out of life's tough times, who never consider the spiritual aspects of problems. Some actually consider it "paranoid" to think that there are spiritual forces behind situations. I have worked with wonderful individuals who, by psychiatric standards of mental disorders, might be considered "disturbed" because they perceived evil spirits or unusual negative thinking behind people's actions. After deeper and lengthier time with these particular patients, it became spiritually clear that they were operating discerning of spirits. This manifestation was one of their spiritual strengths that enabled them to see behind the scenes and to understand spiritual forces underlying external behaviors. Once they learned of their spiritual abilities, fears dissipated. Their lives took on a healthier emotional richness and vitality that continued to sustain them in day-to-day circumstances.

Endnote

crisis: *krima, krino*

The Greek words *crisis*, *krima*, and *krino* are very similar in meaning.

krima means, "condemnation, judgment, damnation." In discussing the qualities of a leader, Paul states, "Not a novice [new convert], lest being lifted up with pride, he fall into condemnation [*krima*] of [by] the devil (I Timothy 3:6)." "Whatsoever is sold in the shambles, that eat, asking no question [*anakrino*] for conscience sake: For the earth is the Lord's and the fullness thereof (I Cor. 10: 25-26) ."

diakrino is "to doubt, stagger at, discern, waver, partiality." "He [Abraham] staggered [*diakrino*] not at the promise of God through unbelief; but was strong in faith, giving glory to God (Romans 4:20) ."

hypokrinomai is "to feign, pretend, act on a stage, judge, under a mask." "And they [the chief priests and scribes] watched him [Jesus], and sent forth spies, which should feign [*hupokrinomai*] themselves just men, that they might take hold of his words, that so they might deliver him unto the power and authority of the governor (Luke 20:20)."

17

OB #4: CONVERSATION OBLIVION

The oblivion of conversation is consistently giving value to communication with the world MORE THAN OR INSTEAD OF communication with God through prayer, the Scriptures, and conversations with other likeminded believers.

Conversation consciousness solution: Consistently giving value to communicating with God through prayer, the Scriptures, and conversations with other likeminded believers MORE THAN OR INSTEAD OF valuing communication with the world.

The Apostle Paul warned that some believers "erred concerning the faith" because they professed things related to the world and science more than spiritual matters.

I Timothy 6:20-21:

O Timothy, keep that which is committed to thy trust [the Word of God concerning Christ], avoiding profane and vain babblings, and oppositions of science falsely so called:

Which some professing [confessing] have erred concerning the faith [have missed the mark concerning the Scriptures regarding Christ]. Grace be with thee. Amen.

It is futile to have dissension over words and issues that contradict the Word of God.

> II Timothy 2:14-16:
>
> Of these things [concerning Christ] put them in remembrance, charging them before the Lord that they strive not about words to no profit [of no value; in vain; virtue-less), but to the subverting [distracting] of the hearers.
>
> STUDY [invest time and energy] to shew thyself approved unto God [to prove to yourself that you are already approved by God], a workman that needeth not to be ashamed, rightly dividing the word of truth.
>
> But SHUN profane and vain babblings; for they will increase unto more ungodliness.

According to these Scriptures, one solution to the irrelevant or bitter use of words is to "study" and "shun." When we *study* the Word of God, we will *shun* vain babblings, such as unprofitable commentaries and senseless questioning, which cause strife.

> II Timothy 2:23:
>
> But foolish and unlearned questions avoid, knowing that they do gender [cause] strife.

People spend most of their waking hours listening to and talking about worldly matters. If one were to evaluate the time and effort spent investing in worldly discussions, it would far outweigh the sharing of spiritual issues.

> *The oblivion of conversation emerges when there is a chronic overloading of all aspects of worldly communication with and about people, places and things.*

This could include an over-abundance of secular reading materials, compulsive media watching, listening to gossip, and fruitless family or work discussions. Even religious gatherings are often bombarded with carnal matters that have nothing to do with God. Nowadays, it is a spiritual battle just to have a simple edifying fellowship with other people centered on the wonderful Word of God. Worldly topics of fear, sickness, worry, death, politics, and humanism constantly threaten to pervade group discussions and the preaching of the Word of God.

I am amazed at how preachers who love God and know a great deal of the Word of God insist on sharing with their congregation the graphic details of politically motivated decisions, and Sister Mary's illness or Brother Jack's recent surgical procedure. Small talk or vain babblings also can go on during formal or informal professional therapeutic interventions. Clinicians who do not recognize or want to understand spiritual issues as vital aspects of evaluation and treatment usually offer time and advice filled with false theoretical and practical worldly solutions. These conversations frequently glorify worldly values and/or self more than the one true God.

> Ephesians 4:29:
>   Let no corrupt communication [rancid words that weaken, negate, water down, or contradict the Word of God] proceed out of your mouth, but that which is good to the use of edifying that it may minister grace unto the hearers.

In our daily discussions inside and outside of work, it is available to bring every topic of concern to the Word of God with or without the use of formal Scriptures. Informal conversations and advice between two people can be wonderful journeys of leading every worldly or carnal thought back to a spiritual understanding of the Word of God. Each misconception, interpersonal contact, and error in thinking can be led captive to the Word of God concerning Christ.

II Corinthians 10:3-5:

For though we walk in the flesh, we do not war after the flesh:

(For the weapons of our warfare are not carnal [fleshly], but mighty through God to the pulling down of strongholds;)

Casting down imaginations, and every high thing that exalteth itself against the knowledge of God, and bringing into captivity every thought to the obedience of Christ.

Which values will we choose in our day-to-day conversations? Will we cast down and hold captive worldly flawed thoughts and try to understand them in the context of the Word of God? Will we walk the path of constant carnal discussions that ultimately set the stage for fear and the oblivion of conversation?

18

LISTENING FOR AN ANSWER

The Scriptures encourage continued dialogue with God rather than the world. We need to listen to God more so that we can manifest the wisdom needed to handle any critical situation. Psalm 46:10 (a) states, "Be still and know that I am God..." There is unspeakable joy in practicing the presence of God in our day-to-day existence.

> Psalm 16:11:
> Thou [God] wilt shew me the path of life: in Thy presence is fullness of joy; at Thy right hand there are pleasures for evermore.

Jesus Christ was the perfect communicator. He remained in constant dialogue with the Father. The Gospel of John, chapter 17, records Jesus' heart wrenching prayer to his Father before he was to be tortured and crucified.

> Verse 4:
> I have glorified thee on the earth: I have finished the work which thou gavest me to do.

> Verse 8 (a):
> I have given unto them the words which thou gavest me...

Verse 25:

O righteous Father, the world hath not known Thee; but I have known Thee, and these have known that Thou hast sent me.

Because of Jesus' obedience unto death, we have greater spiritual consciousness of our direct access to the Father by way of the Holy Spirit.

Ephesians 2:18:

For through him [Jesus Christ] we both [Jew and Gentile] have access by one spirit unto the Father.

If our conversation with God is less frequent, strained, or confused, our relationship with others will be manifested in like fashion. When our "vertical" relationship with God is exercised through frequent and weightier openness with Him, all of our "horizontal" relationships will be handled appropriately, even if the reactions of others may appear negative. God exhorts us to converse with Him, and believe to be inspired to use wisdom in every situation. This is the true spiritual essence of prayer. Turning to Him in any form of prayer or thanksgiving for questions and answers is the primary step in handling critical issues in the world. Turning to His Word is also comparable to speaking with and listening to God because The Word is God.

I Thessalonians 5:17:

Pray without ceasing [continually].

Through prayer, God helps us to remain peaceful during times of stress.

Philippians 4:6-7:

Be careful [anxious] for nothing; but in everything by prayer and supplication with thanksgiving let your requests be made known unto God.

And the peace of God, which passeth all understanding, shall keep [guard] your hearts and minds through Christ Jesus.

Before or during a seemingly critical situation, make a conscious non-reactive spiritual decision "not to decide" about any specific course of action. Instead, pray continually for our hearts to be enlightened regarding the true spiritual nature of our current problem. As we attempt to put on the Scriptures in our minds, God will uncover the needed knowledge and wisdom for the situation.

In the Old Testament, King Solomon asked God for wisdom above all else. As a result, God not only gave him wisdom and knowledge but also great wealth.

II Chronicles 1:6-12:
And Solomon went up thither to the brasen altar before the Lord, which was at the tabernacle of the congregation, and offered a thousand burnt offerings upon it.

In that night did God appear unto Solomon, and said to him, Ask what I shall give thee.

And Solomon said unto God, Thou hast shewed great mercy unto David my father, and hast made me to reign in his stead.

Now, O Lord God, let thy promises unto David my father be established: for thou hast made me king over a people like the dust of the earth in multitude.

Give me now wisdom and knowledge, that I may go out and come in before this people: for who can judge this thy people, that is so great?

And God said to Solomon, Because this was in thine heart, and thou hast not asked riches, wealth, or honour, nor the life of thine enemies, neither yet has asked long life; but hast asked wisdom and knowledge for thyself, that thou mayest judge my people, over whom I have made thee king:

Wisdom and knowledge is granted unto thee; and I will give thee riches, and wealth, and honour, such as none of the kings have had that have been before thee, neither shall there any after thee have the like.

19

SPIRITUALLY BASED PRAYER

Most of the prayers in Paul's seven Church Epistles are heartfelt requests for spiritual wisdom and enlightenment.

Ephesians 1:16-19:

Cease not to give thanks for you, making mention of you in my prayers;

That the God of our Lord Jesus Christ, the Father of glory, may give unto you the Spirit of wisdom and revelation in the knowledge of him:

The eyes of your understanding [heart] being enlightened; that ye may know what is the hope of his calling, and what the riches of the glory of his inheritance in the saints.

And what is the exceeding greatness of his power to usward who believe, according to the working of his mighty power.

Ephesians 3:16-19:

That He [God] would grant you, according to the riches of His glory, to be strengthened with might by His spirit in the inner man;

That Christ may dwell in your hearts by faith; that ye, being rooted and grounded in love,

May be able to comprehend with all the saints what is the breadth, and length, and depth and height [of love];

And to know the love of Christ, which passeth knowledge, that ye might be filled with all the fullness of God.

Colossians 1:9:
For this cause we also, since the day we heard it, do not cease to pray for you, and to desire that ye might be filled with the knowledge of his will in all wisdom and spiritual understanding.

All of these prayers in Ephesians and Colossians are not simply the specific prayers of Paul but spiritual realities that we can consider and request throughout our day.

Jesus taught a parable regarding the importance of continued prayer. It was about a widow who was so persistent that the judge handling her case was forced to resolve her problem. So too, when we persevere in our requests, God is always willing and able to handle our concerns.

Luke 18:1-8(a):
And he spake a parable unto them to this end, that men ought always to pray, and not to faint [in their minds];
Saying, There was in a city a judge, which feared not God, neither regarded [respected] man:
And there was a widow in that city; and she came unto him, saying, Avenge me of mine adversary.
And he would not for a while; but afterward he said within himself,
Though I fear not God, nor regard man;
Yet because this widow troubleth me, I will avenge her, lest by her continual coming [persistence], she weary me.
And the Lord said, Hear what the unjust judge saith.

And shall not God avenge his own elect, which cry day and night [pray incessantly] unto him, though He bear long with them?

I tell you that He will avenge them speedily [at once]

God reminds us that prayer is profitable because He is our Father and we are righteous and valued in His sight.

James 5:16(b):

…The effectual fervent prayer of a righteous man availeth [profits] much.

Heartfelt prayer to God as our Father is spiritually fortified when we use *the name of Jesus Christ*. We have power and authority in that name above all names.

John 16:23:

Whatsoever ye shall ask the Father in my name, He will give it [to] you.

Mark 16:17-18:

And these signs shall follow them that believe; In my name shall they cast out devils; they shall speak with new tongues;

[If] They shall take up serpents; and if they drink any deadly thing, it shall not hurt them; they shall lay hands on the sick, and they shall recover.

Ephesians 5:20:

Giving thanks always for all things unto God and the Father in the name of our Lord Jesus Christ.

Prayer consciousness strategies for supremely valuing God:

❖ Converse directly with Abba, Father

❖ Pray in the name of Jesus Christ

❖ Pray with thanksgiving for what we already have in Christ

❖ Praise and boast of God in, but not for, negative situations

❖ Seek knowledge of the Word concerning prayer

❖ Pray in line with God's Word concerning the crucified, resurrected, and victorious Christ

❖ Pray without ceasing

❖ Carefully read I Corinthians, Chapters 12-14 regarding "speaking in tongues"

❖ Speak in tongues often in private prayer

❖ Ask for forgiveness in order to return to correct thinking and fellowship with God

❖ Take appropriate spiritual actions based upon what God wisely reveals to us in prayer

20

SPEAKING IN TONGUES

Another area to honestly explore and discuss with God through the Scriptures is the role and function of the manifestation of *speaking in tongues*. Some of these issues were discussed in the chapter on the **oblivion of discerning**. The world and many believers are often faced with the question of whether or not God values speaking in tongues. Speaking in tongues is a language unknown to the speaker and is the outward evidence that Christ is in us by way of the Holy Spirit. Speaking in tongues is a manifestation of the Holy Spirit (I Cor. 12: 10) and is "giving thanks well" to God (I Cor. 14:17). It is perfect conversation with God because it bypasses our understanding. There are many times in harsh situations when I do not know exactly what to do or pray for, so I simply speak in the Spirit to God.

> I Corinthians 14:14-15:
> For if I pray in an unknown tongue, my spirit prayeth, but my understanding is unfruitful.
> What is it then? I will pray with the Spirit, and I will pray with the understanding also: I will sing with the Spirit, and I will sing with the understanding also.

> Romans 8:26:
> Likewise the Spirit also helpeth our infirmities: for we know not what we should pray for as we ought: but the Spirit itself maketh intercession for us with groanings which cannot be uttered.

I Corinthians 14:2:

For he that speaketh in an unknown tongue speaketh not unto men, but unto God: for no man understandeth him; howbeit in the Spirit he speaketh mysteries.

Speaking in tongues IS speaking to God.

The ***oblivion of conversation*** can persist when our prayers and conversations with God take a secondary position to valuing feedback from others. Indeed, a life without prayer is a life in ***crisis***. It is "like a boat without an oar." Hebrews, Chapter 13, captures the futility of conversations that are overloaded with the world. However, spiritually based statements and dialogue can shift our balance of values so that we can avoid a ***crisis of conversation***.

Verses 5-8:

Let your conversation be without covetousness [without wanting more from yourself or from the person you are speaking to]; and be content with such things as you have:

For he hath said. I WILL NEVER LEAVE THEE, NOR FORSAKE THEE.

So that we may boldly say [confess] THE LORD IS MY HELPER, AND I WILL NOT FEAR WHAT MAN SHALL DO UNTO ME [We yearn to be in a position of saying what God can do instead of fixating upon wanting more from the systems of the world].

Remember them which have the rule over you, who have spoken unto you the word of God: whose faith follow, considering the end of their conversation. Jesus Christ the same yesterday, and to day, and forever.

Overloading our conversations in the direction of God and His Son, Jesus Christ, will keep us spiritually detached from negative talk that has no spiritual profit.

Conversation oblivion solution: Consistently give value to communicating with God through prayer, the Scriptures, and conversations with other likeminded believers MORE THAN OR INSTEAD OF valuing communication with the world.

__Conversation consciousness strategies:__

- ❖ Preach the Word, whenever possible
- ❖ Bring the Word into mindless or unprofitable conversations
- ❖ Speak the truth in love
- ❖ Continue biblical research with others through *WORD-SHOPS*
- ❖ Relentlessly share the Word concerning Christ
- ❖ Lead every worldly conversation captive to the Word
- ❖ Continually thank God for the wisdom and compassion to minister to the hearts of people through the Word
- ❖ Take valiant action on what God has revealed to you through the Word shared by other believers
- ❖ Continue to re-read and consider the verses in this chapter

PART V
WORSHIP OBLIVION OF THE WORD OF GOD

Worship oblivion can be manifested as it relates to the Word of God. It is a serious lack of spiritual understanding of the Scriptures. There are three subtypes of worship-Word oblivion. All three subtypes involve man's spiritual unawareness of the accuracy, integrity, practical use, and outreach of God's wonderful Word.

Incongruence oblivion: occurs when man places value on an intellectual understanding of the Scriptures and/or private interpretation of the Bible MORE THAN OR INSTEAD OF valuing true spiritual consciousness of the full Gospel of Christ, man's inherent divine nature, and his completeness in Christ.

Integrity oblivion: involves giving value to the world's false portrayal of truth, facts, and religious rituals MORE THAN OR INSTEAD OF valuing a spiritual understanding of the accuracy and integrity of the Word of God.

Research oblivion: researching the accuracy, integrity and spiritual truth of the Word of God MORE THAN OR INSTEAD OF accepting the world's intellectual view of the Bible with its private and religious interpretations.

21

OB #5: INCONGRUENCE OBLIVION

The oblivion of incongruence occurs when the individual places value on five-sense ideas and private interpretation regarding certain aspects of the Scriptures MORE THAN OR INSTEAD OF valuing spiritual consciousness of the meaning and practice of the full Gospel of Christ, man's Divine nature, and his completeness in Christ.

Congruence consciousness solution: Pursuit of spiritual consciousness and practice of the full Gospel of Christ (including his life, Word, crucifixion, resurrection, ascension, and the work of "The Comforter") MORE THAN OR INSTEAD OF maintaining a distorted and incongruent five-sense understanding of biblical ideas and practice.

Jesus Christ often taught his disciples in parables so that they could know the mysteries of the kingdom of God and appreciate how God opens their eyes and ears spiritually.

Matthew 13:10-17:

And the disciples came and said unto him, Why speakest thou unto them in parables? He answered and said unto them, Because it is given unto you to know the mysteries of the kingdom of heaven, but to them it is not given.

For whosoever hath, to him shall be given, and shall have more abundance: but whosoever hath not, from him shall be taken away even that he hath.

Therefore speak I to them in parables: because they seeing see not [spiritually]; and hearing they hear not [spiritually], neither do they understand.

In them is fulfilled the prophecy of Esaias [Isaiah], which saith, BY HEARING YE SHALL HEAR, AND SHALL NOT UNDERSTAND; AND SEEING YE SHALL SEE, AND SHALL NOT PERCEIVE: FOR THIS PEOPLE'S HEART IS WAXED GROSS [CALLOUS], AND THEIR EARS ARE DULL OF HEARING, AND THEIR EYES THEY HAVE CLOSED; LEST AT ANY TIME THEY SHOULD SEE WITH THEIR EYES AND HEAR WITH THEIR EARS, AND SHOULD UNDERSTAND WITH THEIR HEART, AND SHOULD BE CONVERTED [TURNED TOWARD GOD], AND I SHOULD HEAL THEM.

But blessed are your eyes, for they see: and your ears, for they hear.

For verily I say unto you, That many prophets and righteous men have desired to see those things which ye see, and have not seen them; and to hear those things which ye hear, and have not heard them.

In the Gospels (Matthew 13; Mark 4; Luke 8), Jesus discussed the parable of the "sower and the seed," which exemplifies how spiritual consciousness of the Word becomes distorted because of worldly or egotistic distractions.

Luke 8:5-8(a):

A sower went out to sow his seed: and as he sowed, some fell by the way side; and it was trodden down, and the fowls of the air devoured it.

And some fell upon a rock; and as soon as it was sprung up, it withered away, because it lacked moisture.

And some fell among thorns; and the thorns sprang up with it, and choked it.

And other fell on good ground, and sprang up, and bare fruit an hundred fold...

In Luke 8:11-15, Jesus provided the interpretation of this parable.

Now the parable [of the sower and the seed] is this: The seed is the Word of God.

Those by the way side are they that hear [the Word of God]; then cometh the devil, and taketh away the word out of their hearts, lest they should believe and be saved.

They [that fell] on the rock are they, which, when they hear, receive the word with joy; and these have no root, which for a while believe, and in time of temptation [persecution; pressure] fall away. And that [seed] which fell among thorns are they, which, when they have heard, go forth, and are choked with the cares and riches and pleasures of this life, and bring no fruit to perfection.

But that [seed] on good ground are they which in an honest and good heart, having heard the word, keep it, and bring forth fruit with patience.

According to this parable, there are four different critical responses to the Word of God. The first three responses are errors in thinking and reflect incongruence between spiritual consciousness and practice of the true Word. The fourth response reflects "true spiritual consciousness and congruent practice of God's unalterable Word."

1) *Wayside Word Incongruence*: An individual hears some of the Word of God but has no spiritual consciousness of the meaning. Consequently, immediately it is snatched away and he remains in a world of mortal thinking. The result is that the person does not know enough of, distorts or forgets the Word. This condition is a serious spiritual ***crisis of worship*** that can only be spiritually resolved when he comes to Christ and grows in spiritual understanding of his inherent divine nature.

2. *Rocky Word Incongruence*: An individual hears the Word joyfully. But there is no root in his heart (a lack of spiritual consciousness of the meaning of the Word). When pressure comes, the Word falls away.

3. *Thorny Word Incongruence*: An individual hears the Word; however, because of worldly cares, riches, and pleasures, he becomes spiritually confused and the Word is choked.

4. *Good Ground Word Congruence*: The fourth response to the Word reflects a true spiritual congruence of understanding and practice of the Word. Spiritual man hears, spiritually understands, and keeps the Word in his heart. By God's grace and mercy, he maintains consistent values in the direction of the Word of God instead of the world. As a result, he lives the Word, practices God's presence, and spiritual fruit is brought forth with patience. In this condition, there is a significant amount of understanding of the Word of God in the mind, heart ("good ground") and action patterns of the believer so as to outweigh and counteract the world's pressures and pleasures. There is no *crisis*.

Incongruence oblivion solution: Pursue spiritual consciousness and practice of the full Gospel of Christ

(including his life, Word, crucifixion, resurrection, ascension, and the work of "The Comforter") MORE THAN OR INSTEAD OF maintaining a distorted and incongruent five-sense understanding of biblical ideas and practice.

Oblivion of Incongruence Success Strategies:

➤ Seek spiritual understanding of the scriptures on this chapter

➤ Allow the Word to dwell in your heart and mind

➤ Take appropriate action on the Word you have been taught

➤ Practice what you preach

➤ Preach what you practice

➤ Lead every thought and action captive to God's Word

➤ By God's grace, pursue a spiritual balance between spiritual understanding and wise action

22

OB #6: INTEGRITY OBLIVION

The oblivion of integrity exists when we continually listen to, value, and accept legalistic, private, interpretations of the Bible MORE THAN OR INSTEAD OF the spiritual accuracy and integrity of the Word of God.

Solution: Researching the accuracy, integrity and spiritual truth of the Word of God MORE THAN OR INSTEAD OF accepting the world's intellectual view of the Bible with its private and religious interpretations.

The systems of the world often address the importance of integrity in all areas of life. Individuals are thought to have integrity by being honest in their dealings and keeping their promises. According to *Merriam-Webster's Dictionary*, "integrity" means, "soundness; a firm adherence to a code of moral or artistic values; the quality or state of being complete."

The world speaks of facts, opinions, and commentaries as though they are truth. People have said, "Well, that's the truth of the situation." "I am only telling you the truth." The question is: What is truth? In John 14:6, Jesus Christ said, "...I am the way, the truth and the life. No man comes unto the Father but by me." John 17:17 states that God's Word is truth. "Sanctify them through Thy truth: Thy word is truth." The Holy Spirit also is truth.

John 16:13-14:

> Howbeit, when he, the Spirit of truth, is come, he will
> guide you into all truth: for he shall not speak of himself;
> but whatsoever he shall hear, that shall he speak: and he
> shall show you things to come.
>
> He shall glorify me [Jesus Christ]: for he shall receive
> of mine, and shall shew it unto you.

If spiritual man continues to think and act in line with the accurate Word
of God, he shall know the truth.

John 8:31-32:

> Then said Jesus to those Jews which believed on him,
> If ye continue in my word, then are ye my disciples indeed;
>
> And ye shall know the truth, and the truth [of the
> Word of God] shall make you free.

So-called truths propounded by the world should never contradict the
Word of God. Worldly facts can never negate the truth of Jesus Christ, the
reality of the Holy Spirit, and the unconditional love of God.

Biblical research of the Greek word, *crisis*, provides insight into the
integrity and soundness of the Word of God.

Hebrews 4:12:

> For the Word of God is quick [alive; living], and
> powerful, and sharper than any two-edged sword, piercing
> even to the dividing asunder of soul and spirit, and of the
> joints and marrow, and is a discerner [*kritikos*] of the
> thoughts and intents of the heart.

The Greek word, *kritikos,* comes from the word, *crisis*, and is synonymous
with the English words, "critic," "critical," and "discerner." The Word of

God is the critic. It is the primary standard for truth-filled living. The Word helps us to spiritually and mentally perceive what is going on in our lives. It encourages us to accept that we are eternally valued. As spiritual beings created in God's image, and further enlightened by Christ and The Holy Spirit, God speaks to us through the Scriptures. The Word of God does "heart surgery." It enables us to see what is in our hearts. Through the wisdom of the Holy Spirit, our hearts can be molded to track with the Scriptures.

> *Consistently using the accurate Word of God as the primary standard for truth will help to us avert the oblivion of integrity.*

After hearing the Apostle Paul preach Christ and the resurrection, the Jews in the synagogue at Berea searched and researched the Scriptures for their accuracy and integrity. They carefully looked for and evaluated any discrepancies between what the leader said and what the Word of God proclaimed.

> Acts 17:10-11:
>
> And the brethren immediately sent away Paul and Silas by night unto Berea: who coming thither went into the synagogue of the Jews.
>
> These were more noble [had greater concern for character and values in the Word] than those in Thessalonica, in that they received the Word [of God] with all readiness of mind, and searched the Scriptures daily [continually], whether those things were so.

The word, "searched," comes from the Greek word, *anakrino*, which is related to the word, *crisis*. It means, "not to intellectually examine the Scriptures but to rely upon the Holy Spirit to teach and instruct." These

Bereans were trusting God to help them to spiritually understand the accuracy and integrity of the Bible.

I Corinthians 2:14:

But the natural man [five senses man without consciousness of his divine spiritual identity] receiveth not the things of the Spirit of God: for they are foolishness unto him: neither can he know them, because they are spiritually discerned [*anakrino*].

Searching the Scriptures takes time, effort, a willingness of mind, and instruction from other informed believers. Only God can teach and help us to spiritually understand the meaning of the Scriptures.

I John 2:27:

But the anointing [The Holy Spirit in manifestation] which ye have received of him abideth in you, and ye need not that any man teach you: but as the same anointing teacheth you of all things, and is truth, and is no lie, and even as it hath taught you, you shall abide in him.

God exhorts us to study and research His Word concerning Christ who is "the Word made flesh;" he embodied the fullness of the Word.

John 1:14:

And the Word was made flesh, and dwelt among us, (and we beheld his glory, the glory as of the only begotten of the Father,) full of grace and truth.

To counterbalance the usual bombardment of worldly values and information, we continually receive the Word with meekness, apply it in our lives, share it with others, and fellowship with those who enjoy the same Word.

II Timothy 2:15:

Study [invest time and energy] to shew thyself approved unto God, a workman who needeth not be ashamed, rightly dividing the word of truth [the Word of God].

Research of the Word of God is absolutely profitable and valuable. It enables us to be "prepared unto all good works."

II Timothy 3:16-17:

All scripture is given by inspiration of God [God-breathed], and is profitable [valuable] for doctrine, for reproof, for correction, for instruction in righteousness [right living]: That the man of God [anyone who speaks the accuracy of God's Word for Him] may be perfect, throughly furnished [prepared] unto all good [valuable] works.

The more time we spend in the world, the more likely we will be out of harmony and think in the direction of the world's values. Increased exposure to the world's systems will require greater amounts of the Word of God to shift to spiritual values toward Christ. If we do not know that we need to shift values, the *oblivion of integrity* probably already exists or is looming. We will need to consistently "put on the whole armour of God" by giving greater weight and value to the Word of God, prayer, and fellowshipping with others.

Ephesians 6:10-18 unfolds significant elements of this "spiritual armour."

Finally, my brethren, be strong in the Lord and in the power of his might.

Put on the whole armour of God, that ye may be able to stand against the wiles of the devil.

For we wrestle not against flesh and blood, but against principalities, against powers, against the rulers of the darkness of this world, against spiritual wickedness in high places.

Wherefore take unto you the whole armour of God, that ye may be able to withstand in the evil day, and having done all, to stand.

Stand therefore, having your loins girt about with truth [the Word of God], and having on the breastplate of righteousness [the reality that you are righteous, valued, and worthy in Christ];

And your feet shod with the preparation of the Gospel of peace;

Above all, taking the shield of faith [the believing ability of Jesus Christ, which is in you by way of the gift of the Holy Spirit], wherewith ye shall be able to quench all the fiery darts of the wicked.

And take the helmet of salvation, and the sword of the Spirit, which is the Word of God:

Praying always with all prayer and supplication in the Spirit, and watching thereunto with all perseverance and supplication for all the saints.

Consciousness integrity solution: Researching the accuracy, integrity and spiritual truth of the Word of God MORE THAN OR INSTEAD OF accepting the world's intellectual view of the Bible with its private and religious interpretations.

23

OB #7: RESEARCH OBLIVION

If we rigorously want to seek the spiritual truth of the Word, we will need instruction and practice on how to research it so as to increase spiritual consciousness.

❖ **Study the Word of God concerning Christ.** Learn to read and apply biblical principles and Scriptures on your own so as to reduce dependency on anyone else but God. The full Gospel of Christ needs to be explored. Try not to focus on only one aspect of Christ. Partial knowledge of the Scriptures concerning Christ can sustain *research oblivion*. Pursue aspects of your own history or specific elements of critical situations, and ask God for spiritual understanding as you read each verse and paragraph of the Word.

❖ **Watch for and listen to contradictions between your particular situation and the Word of God.** Be conscious of the spiritual battle and the need to ask God for wisdom. It is vital that we know when the integrity of the Word of God concerning Christ has been compromised, watered down, or completely changed.

The entire Bible from Genesis to Revelation is the "word of truth." It prophesizes and describes events regarding the first coming of Christ, his life, his second coming, and the final judgment of God. Through rigorous research of the seven Church Epistles, we attain greater clarity regarding various passages of the Old and New Testaments concerning the righteousness of God. The Old Testament tells us that we have to work for our righteousness, whereas the New Testament reminds us to work out or manifest the righteousness by grace we already received through

Christ. Although a deeper scope of Christ and his righteousness begins with the prophecies of him throughout the Old Testament and ends in the final Book of Revelation, believers in Christ would find it profitable to spend periods of time understanding the Gospels and the Church Epistles concerning our divine nature.

Suggested Order of Studying the Word for Greater Spiritual Understanding:

READ FIRST: The seven Church Epistles (Romans through I and II Thessalonians), the Pastoral Epistles (I and II Timothy, Titus, and Philemon), and the Epistles that follow (Hebrews, James, I and II Peter, and I, II, and III John). These Epistles unfold the reality of our divine nature.

READ SECOND: The Book of Acts, which tells of the Holy Spirit on the day of Pentecost, and provides specific examples of the "actions of the Holy Spirit" in the lives of spiritual men and women.

READ THIRD: The Four Gospels of Matthew, Mark, Luke, and John. These books report the significance of Jesus' life, death on the cross, resurrection, and ascension. Recognizing these realities is vital for our understanding of the spiritual righteousness we have in Christ. This righteousness by grace does not stop at the cross and with information provided in the Four Gospels, but continues in the Church Epistles regarding the glorious return of Christ.

READ FOURTH: Psalms, Proverbs, and other books of the Old Testament (i.e., Jeremiah, Daniel, Isaiah) provide the backdrop for the coming Messiah, the Christ. Read these books from the perspective of the seven Church Epistles and the Four Gospels. The words of "the Comforter" found in the Epistles are specifically addressed to spiritually enlightened man.

A significant source of confusion regarding the use of Scriptures is the wrong or private interpretation of the Bible. This occurs because well-meaning people have been wrongly taught concerning the finished work of Christ. If we do not know or believe what God accomplished in Christ, we can readily move from neurotic despair to a debilitating mortal condition.

Often, a believer evidences **oblivion of research** when he makes constant worldly statements that contradict the Word of God. As fellow-believers, we want to minister to him. We believe God to hear the man's errors in thinking or imbalances of values toward the world in order to say to this pained individual, *"That's not what the Word of God says. The God you are talking about is not the God and Father of Jesus Christ. He is not the God I know from the Scriptures."*

Recently, in one short conversation I had with an acquaintance at a health club, she made three inaccurate statements about God and the Bible. These statements included: *"God helps those who help themselves." "I have my own private religion." "I don't preach what I believe."* All of these simplistic responses contradict the Word of God. The biblical reality is that God helps those who seek His help and help others. God also wants us to openly preach and teach the Word of God concerning Christ.

> II Timothy 4:2(a):
>> Preach the Word; be instant in season, out of season [Always look for an opportunity to share the Word of God]...

Diligent study of the Scriptures prepares us for spiritual and critical battles, no matter how big or small. Seeking God's help to "renew our minds" to the Word of God enables us to be inspired, think correctly, and make wise spiritual decisions.

Romans 12:1-2:

I beseech you therefore, brethren, by the mercies of God, that ye present your bodies a living sacrifice, holy, acceptable unto God, which is your reasonable service.

And be not conformed to this world; but be ye transformed [molded by God] by the RENEWING OF YOUR MIND, that ye may prove what is that good, and acceptable, and perfect will of God.

According to I Corinthians 2:11-16, an individual can only comprehend the Scriptures if he has true spiritual understanding. With a divine nature, he accepts that he has "the mind of Christ" spiritually and is able to receive spiritual information.

But what man knoweth the things of man, save [except by] the spirit of man which is in him? Even so the things of God knoweth no man, but the Spirit of God.

Now we have received, not the spirit of the world, but the spirit which is of God, that we might know the things that are freely given to us of God.

Which things also we speak, not in the words which man's wisdom teacheth, but which the Holy Ghost [Holy Spirit] teacheth, comparing spiritual things with spiritual.

But the natural man [the five senses man; the man who is unaware of his divine nature] receiveth not the things of the Spirit of God: for they are foolishness unto him: neither can he know them, because they are spiritually discerned.

But he that is spiritual judgeth all things, yet he himself is judged of no man.

For WHO HATH KNOWN THE MIND OF THE
LORD, THAT HE MAY INSTRUCT HIM? But we
have the mind of Christ [spiritually].

God wants us to attend to and meditate upon Him and His Word.

I Timothy 4:13, 15-16:
Till I come, give attendance to reading, to exhortation,
to doctrine [the Word of God].
Meditate upon these things [the Word of God]; give
thyself wholly unto them; that thy profiting may appear
unto all.
Take heed to thyself, and unto the doctrine [the Word
of God]; continue in them: for in doing this thou shalt
save thyself, and them that hear thee.

***The primary key to dealing with Word-based spiritual
oblivion is to allow the Word of God concerning Christ
to dwell in us. The Word spiritually admonishes and
counsels us, and sets the foundation for what is to be
valued.***

Colossians 3:16:
Let [allow] the Word of Christ dwell in you richly
in all wisdom teaching and admonishing one another in
psalms and hymns and spiritual songs, singing with grace
in your hearts to the Lord.

We are to receive God's Word to the point of being continually conscious
of His presence and boldly acting upon what He tells us by inspiration or
revelation.

James 1:21-22:

Wherefore lay apart [put off] all filthiness and superfluity of naughtiness [abundance of evil], and receive with meekness the engrafted [implanted] word which is able to save your souls.

But be ye doers of the word, and not hearers only, deceiving your own selves.

A great deception is to intellectually study the Scriptures but not to seek spiritual understanding and application. This cerebral approach to the Word of God will keep us in fear, doubt, and worry. As a result, we can become deceived into turning to the world with its principles and theories for answers. This ought not to be. It is vital that we remain spiritually aware of worldly traditions and theories that move us away from Christ and our completeness in him.

Colossians 2:8-10:

Beware lest any man spoil you through philosophy and vain deceit, after the traditions of men, after the rudiments [principles] of the world, and not after Christ.

For in him dwelleth all the fullness of the Godhead bodily.

And ye are complete in him, which is the head of all principality and power.

Research Oblivion Solution: Research the accuracy, integrity and spiritual truth of the Word of God MORE THAN OR INSTEAD OF accepting the world's intellectual view of the Bible with its private and religious interpretations.

Spiritually conscious research strategies:

For a true and accurate spiritually based study of the Scriptures, pursue the following:

- ❖ Pray to God to grow in grace
- ❖ Consider the verses in this and other chapters of the book
- ❖ Read with a purpose or a question in mind
- ❖ Study and meditate on a verse or verses
- ❖ Read the context of a verse (within the chapter, and in the chapters before and after)
- ❖ Do a "Word study" on a specific word or phrase
- ❖ Use a concordance for further understanding of biblical word usages
- ❖ Study the culture of the times; research old biblical locations and customs
- ❖ Focus on the four Gospels and the seven Church Epistles (Romans through Thessalonians). Together, they reflect the full Gospel of Christ. His words and the words regarding the Holy Spirit are specifically addressed to spiritually enlightened man

PART VI
WORSHIP OBLIVION OF ONE'S SPIRITUAL WORTH

There are four additional subtypes of worship oblivion that involve man's thoughts and actions regarding himself, namely, sin consciousness, blinded spiritual sense of true righteousness, worldly hopelessness, and confused idol worship of self and/or others. All four subtypes lack spiritual awareness of man's worthiness created in God's image (Genesis 1:26-27).

Condemnation oblivion is maintaining a deceived mental state of spiritual unworthiness and sin-consciousness MORE THAN OR INSTEAD OF being spiritually conscious that man is and has always been a spiritual being created in God's image. This oblivion can result in a deep sense of sorrow, loss, suicidal ideation, and depression.

Righteousness oblivion is the consistently deceptive valuing of self-righteousness, false humility and/or pride INSTEAD OF one's permanent righteousness in God through Christ. This oblivion can cause natural critical dilemmas such as illness, failed relationships, disappointment, over-indulgence, and legalistic religious practices.

Hope oblivion is consistently and hopelessly valuing the fear of death, preparation for death, and living from moment to moment by the world's standards of the future MORE THAN OR INSTEAD OF accepting that we already have eternal life and look forward to the future return of Christ. Manifestations of this oblivion can include despair, excessive death preoccupation, fear of aging, vanity, anxious preparation for death, and fixation with the hereafter.

Example/comparison oblivion is a chronic spiritual condition of valuing status, examples, and role models from the world MORE THAN OR INSTEAD OF Christ who is THE EXAMPLE and role model for all time. The outcome of this oblivion often is jealousy and unhealthy competition.

24

OB #8: CONDEMNATION OBLIVION

The oblivion of (mental) condemnation is valuing a deceived mental state of unworthiness and "valuelessness" MORE THAN OR INSTEAD OF accepting the reality that man is a spiritual being created in God's image. Man falsely believes that, as a result of Adam's disobedience, he lost permanent spiritual worthiness and fellowship with God. The spiritual truth is that he lives in a chronic state of mental condemnation, sin-consciousness and sustained low or false esteem.

Condemnation consciousness solution: Man pursues spiritual consciousness regarding his inherent divine nature of worth MORE THAN OR INSTEAD OF accepting a state of mental sin-consciousness and perceived loss of connection with God.

Mortal man does not understand or accept his worth-ship as a spiritual being. Consequently, he is motivated by a deep sense of mental condemnation and sin-consciousness.

Throughout the New Testament, we immediately recognize the significance of Jesus Christ as God's only solution to the *oblivion of mental condemnation* faced by every individual in this world. The Gospel of John is replete with references to man's persistent sense of condemnation [*crisis*]. In the Gospel of John, Chapter 3, Jesus spoke of God's tremendous love for people and His concern with the world's critical state of affairs.

John 3:16-20:

For God so loved the world that he gave his only begotten Son, that whosoever believeth in him should not perish but have everlasting life.

For God sent not his Son into the world to condemn the world; but that the world through him might be saved [made whole].

He that believeth on him [Jesus Christ] is not condemned; but he that believeth not is condemned already [remains in the *oblivion of condemnation*], because he hath not believed in [is not spiritually conscious of] the name of the only begotten Son of God.

This is the condemnation [the *oblivion of condemnation*], that light is come into the world and men loved [were deceived into loving] darkness rather than [instead of] light, because their deeds were evil.

For everyone that doeth evil hateth the light, neither cometh to the light, lest his deeds should be reproved [examined; evaluated].

The oblivion of condemnation is that men continue to value darkness INSTEAD OF the light, God, His Son, Jesus Christ, the written Word of God, and the Holy Spirit.

All mortal men and women automatically value darkness (non-light; non-Christ) rather than Jesus Christ who is "the light of the world" (John 8:12). By omission or commission, they pursue darkness instead of the Word of God, which is "a light unto my path" (Psalm 119:105). This is the basic mental condition of man, unless or until he comes to the enlightened spiritual reality of his inherent divine nature and his completeness in Christ. The only way to walk out of the darkened mental crisis of the soul, a deep and mistaken sense of *condemnation,* is to come to the "light of life," Jesus Christ, who provided spiritual understanding and uplifted consciousness of the written and spoken Word of God.

> John 8:12:
>
> Then spake Jesus again unto them, saying, I am the light of the world: he that followeth me shall not walk in darkness, but shall have the light of life.

> John 5:24:
>
> Verily, verily, I [Jesus Christ] say unto you, he that heareth my word, and believeth on him that sent me, hath everlasting life, and shall not come into [remain in] [mental] condemnation but is passed from death to life.

Without a conscious knowledge of and conviction to our spiritual valueness, all of mortal man remains in spiritual oblivion. When we become spiritually conscious of Christ's words and believe in Almighty God who sent him, we are brought out of this *crisis* into the spiritual truth that we already have eternal life.

> I John 5:11:
>
> And this is the record, that God hath given to us eternal life, and this life is in his Son.

> ***Believing in Christ is a spiritual process that begins with God and the actions of the Holy Spirit. Only by God's mercy and grace can anyone become spiritually aware of the light.***

> II Corinthians 4:6:
>
> For God, who commanded the light to shine out of darkness, hath shined in our hearts [spiritually enlightened

our understanding], to give the light of the knowledge of
the glory of God in the face of Jesus Christ.

God has the ultimate power to rescue us from the power of darkness (non-light) and to bring us into the kingdom of His Son, Jesus Christ.

> Colossians 1:13-14:
> Who [God] hath delivered [rescued] us from the power
> of darkness, and hath translated us into the kingdom of
> His dear Son;
> In whom [Jesus Christ] we have redemption [have
> been set free; totally released] through his blood, even the
> forgiveness [a total washing away; full remission] of sins
> [errors in thinking and believing].

God gave Jesus Christ the sole authority to handle the world's spiritual oblivion because he is His only-begotten Son.

> John 5:27:
> And [God] hath given him [Jesus Christ] authority to
> execute judgment [*crisis*] [authority to resolve the *crisis
> of condemnation*] also, because he is the Son of man.

> *Man is always in search of God, whether he realizes this
> spiritual reality or not. Until he becomes spiritually
> conscious of Him through Christ, he will stay critically
> and hopelessly in a mental state of spiritual blindness
> and condemnation.*

The world considers every human being to have choices in life. Without God through Christ, mortal man cannot make spiritually conscious choices. He lives by the standards of the world and is under its domain. Before coming to the reality of their true spiritual identity through Christ, all human beings are motivated by their inner materialistic and mortal values.

The spiritual power of God in raising Jesus Christ from the dead and setting him at His right hand is available to anyone who comes to Christ.

Romans 8:11:

But if [since] the Spirit of him that raised up Jesus from the dead dwell in you, he that raised up Christ from the dead shall also quicken your mortal bodies by his Spirit that dwelleth in you.

As spiritual men and women, we are already seated spiritually in the "heavenlies" looking down at the world's problems.

Ephesians 2:4-6:

But God, who is rich in mercy, for his great love wherewith he loved us,

Even when we were dead in sins, hath quickened us together with Christ, (by grace are you saved;)

And hath raised us up together, and made us sit together in heavenly places in Christ Jesus.

Ephesians 1:19-23:

And what is the exceeding greatness of his [God's] power to usward who believe, according to the working of his mighty power,

Which he wrought in Christ, when he raised him from the dead, and set him at his own right hand in the heavenly places,

Far above all principality, and power, and might, and dominion, and every name that is named, not only in this world, but also in that which is to come; And hath put all things under his feet, and gave him to be the head over all things to the church,

Which is his body, the fullness of him that filleth all in all.

In this day and time, man's personal *crisis of condemnation* continues until he responds to the spiritual enlightenment of God and becomes yoked or balanced with the master. He needs to be joined with "the healer of broken hearts," Jesus Christ, and to know that he is a spiritual being indeed.

Condemnation consciousness solution: Pursue spiritual consciousness regarding man's inherent divine nature of worth and value MORE THAN OR INSTEAD OF accepting a state of mental sin-consciousness and perceived loss of connection with God.

Claim specific consciousness affirmation strategies:

- ❖ There is "now no condemnation" to us who are in Christ Jesus (Romans 8:1)
- ❖ We have eternal life NOW (I John 5:11)
- ❖ We have been created in the image of God (Genesis 1:26-27)
- ❖ When God sees us, he sees "Christ" who is worthy and righteous in His eyes
- ❖ Nothing can separate us from the love of God, which is in Christ Jesus (Romans 8:31-39)

25

OB #9: RIGHTEOUSNESS OBLIVION

The oblivion of righteousness is continually enter-taining chronically mistaken feelings, thoughts, perceptions, and actions of self-righteousness, over-estimation, pride, arrogance and unrighteousness. In this crisis, we repeatedly give value to what the world claims regarding our righteousness MORE THAN or INSTEAD OF accepting the righteousness of God that we have in Christ.

Consciousness of righteousness solution: Accept that we are made righteous with God, and be thankful that we are good enough and free from sin because of God in Christ MORE THAN OR INSTEAD OF looking to the world or ourselves for approval and affirmation of moral rightness.

We need a fuller spiritual understanding of how God made us righteous in Christ. Because of the Word and works of Christ, his crucifixion, resurrection and ascension, we have been spiritually enlightened to God's righteousness in us. We are right with God; we have a spiritual sense of rightness and morality with God. To Him, we are good enough.

I Corinthians 1:30:
> But of him are ye in Christ Jesus who of God is made unto us wisdom, and righteousness, and sanctification [holiness; set apart], and redemption.

As a part of our God-given righteousness, we have been "justified." It is "just as if" we had never sinned. We have been freed from the penalty of sin.

> Romans 3:24:
> Being justified freely by his grace through the redemption that is in Christ Jesus:

When God sees us, he sees the spiritual perfection He created.

> Mathew 5:48:
> Be ye therefore perfect, as your Father in heaven is perfect.

There is a difference between having something spiritually and claiming it mentally and practically in our everyday lives. Although we are already righteous spiritually as reflections of God, we often face taunting mental pressures about our righteousness. People, places, things and false claims from the world constantly try to get us to question, negate, or over-estimate our righteousness.

There is a constant battle in the minds and hearts of spiritual men and women over what to value more…the righteousness we have received by grace or feelings of false self-elevation and pride. The systems of the world continually will lie to us and tell us to believe in ourselves and in none other. Materialistic approaches will use anything and anyone from the present or past to arouse old feelings of self-pride. Slyly, the world will encourage negative thinking regarding situations that occurred before we came to Christ, events for which we have already been freed from the penalty of sin.

In the *oblivion of righteousness*, there are two significant deceptions:

1) ***Deception of arrogance***: We are consistently deceived into accepting exaggerated importance of ourselves more than our spiritual righteousness in Christ. Consequently, we find ourselves continually trying to walk by the world's standards more than by the standards of the Word of God concerning Christ.

2) ***Deception of non-change***: We are deceived into thinking and believing that we have not changed and never will. We repeatedly elevate our old arrogant mental and physical habit patterns above our divine nature. Consequently, even after we have been spiritually enlightened of our righteousness by grace, we still end up "walking by the flesh" rather than the Spirit of God.

The Word of God offers instruction on how to renew our minds to true spiritual righteousness.

> II Timothy 3:16:
>
> All scripture [from Genesis to Revelation] is given by inspiration of God and is profitable [valuable] for doctrine [what to think and believe correctly], for reproof [where we have errors in our thinking and believing], for correction [how to get back to right thinking and believing), for [which is] instruction in righteousness.

The seven Church Epistles (Romans through Thessalonians) remind us that we are a "new creature in Christ" (II Cor. 5:17). We are made righteous and complete in Christ (Colossians 2:10). Every materialistic system will tell us that we are too righteous or unrighteous. Everything around us will enhance the thought that we are more important than God or less valued than what God says we are.

Confusion over righteousness occurs because we do not know, have not been taught, or misinterpret the Bible.

We haphazardly go to the Old Testament or the Gospels to confirm our unrighteousness or righteousness "by works."

Often, we have overlooked, swayed away from, or have never been taught the gripping realities of the seven Church Epistles, which are addressed specifically to enlightened spiritual men and women who are already righteous by grace and not by works.

Spiritual man, valued and righteous before God, can and still does sin; but sin is "an error in thinking or believing that affects our ongoing fellowship with God." Flawed mental patterns basically come from not knowing, wrong knowing or not having a spiritual understanding of the Word of God in some area of life.

To sin is to believe the lies and mistakes of the world more than or instead of God.

We have physical bodies and emotions that continue to make us vulnerable to an overload of five-sense information and resulting wrong decisions. It is a continual spiritual challenge to outweigh the senses by strong doses of the Word of God. Romans 6:12 exhorts: "Let not sin [errors in your thought patterns] therefore reign [prevail] in your mortal body, that ye should obey it in the lusts thereof."

26

PERCEIVED UNRIGHTEOUSNESS

When we have errors in thinking, there ought to be "godly sorrow." This kind of sorrow is a spiritual recognition or conviction that we are thinking or acting wrongly.

II Corinthians 7:9, 11:

Now I rejoice, not that ye were made sorry, but that ye sorrowed to repentance: for ye were made sorry after a godly manner, that ye might receive damage by us in nothing.

For behold this selfsame thing, that ye sorrowed after a godly sort, what carefulness [heart-searching] it wrought in you, yea, what clearing of yourselves, yea, what indignation, yea, what fear, what vehement desire, yea, what zeal, yea, what revenge! In all things, ye have approved yourselves to be clear in this matter.

If we refuse to listen to the Holy Spirit and do not confess our sins [errors in thinking or believing] to God, we will maintain feelings of being convicted that can result in chronic condemnation, despair, and un-forgiveness.

I John 1:8:

If we say that we have no sin, we deceive ourselves, and the truth is not in us.

If we do not adhere to the Holy Spirit's conviction and choose not to confess our sins (errors in thinking or believing), we deceive ourselves.

Knowing that we are forgiven for sins is a significant part of reclaiming and maintaining our mental belief and feelings of righteousness. A sense of un-forgiveness builds fear, doubt, and bitterness.

> I John 1:9:
>> If we confess our sins, he is faithful and just to forgive us our sins, and to cleanse us from all unrighteousness.

The phrase, "cleanse us from all unrighteousness," has to do with all unrighteous actions and things done wrong. We can never lose our spiritual righteousness, since we already have been made and forever will remain spiritually righteous with God through Christ.

> II Corinthians 5:21:
>> For he hath made him [Jesus] to be sin for us, who knew no sin; that we might be made the righteousness of God in him.

All of us are faced with issues of "perceived unrighteousness." If this false thinking becomes persistent, it can drive us to repetitive unrighteous living. Not seeking to correct wrong thinking or not consistently renewing the mind to our righteousness will result in a deceived mental state of unrighteousness and condemnation. Ultimately, this continual distortion in thinking and believing manifests itself in spiritual oblivion of one's spiritual righteousness.

> Romans 12:2:
>> And be not conformed to this world: but be ye transformed by the renewing of your mind, that ye may prove what is that good, and acceptable, and perfect, will of God.

The world is designed to judge people by how they behave and what they accomplish. Worldly systems hardly consider the spiritual realities of the Bible and what it says about a believer in Christ. As a result, many of us do not feel valued or may over-estimate ourselves in the world. We feel attractive or successful by worldly or carnal standards. Frequently, we need help during these continued mental episodes of self-righteousness. God wants us to turn to Him and His Son, first and foremost. With the Spirit of God coupled with the availability of the Scriptures, prayer, and encouragement by other believers, there is no reason that we should have to live in the long-term bondage of mental unrighteousness. God always gives us the victory in Christ.

> II Corinthians 2:14(a):
> Now, thanks be unto God, which [who] always causeth us to triumph in Christ...

There are and will be times when neither prayer nor the Scriptures seem to be working. Our minds become confused or "un-renewed" to God's Word. During those episodes, "helping ministries," such as other believers, church leaders, healing professionals or "covalent counselors" (Cosenza, 2008) will be beneficial for practical guidance and instruction in Christ. This is "Christ-is" intervention (Cosenza, 2006).

> I Corinthians 12:28:
> And God hath set some in the church, first apostles, secondarily prophets, thirdly teachers, after that miracles, then gifts of healings, helps [helping ministries], governments, diversities [different kinds] of tongues.

Caring helpers will need to listen carefully to an individual. Any personal information divulged to them needs to be kept secret. It is so true that "loose lips sink ships." Believers in need should expect that a loving listener would not betray a confidence to anyone, except by permission or because of potential serious danger or harm to that person or others. Too often, in the church, listeners of trouble feel compelled to tell information about a believer to the leadership or other believers. Because of this possibility, needy Christians frequently choose to seek out worldly professionals who are not known to their local congregation. This insures privacy and confidentiality. God is unlimited. When needed, He will work with loving clinicians to help a believer feel well enough to return to Him and His Word. There have been many cases of secular therapists who became believers in God and His Son as a result of their experiences in helping God's children.

Consciousness of righteousness solution: Accept that we are made righteous with God, and be thankful that we are good enough and free from sin because of God in Christ MORE THAN OR INSTEAD OF looking to the world or ourselves for approval and affirmation of moral rightness.

Righteousness consciousness intervention/strategies:

- ❖ Claim that you are righteous NOW
- ❖ Accept that your righteousness is by grace alone
- ❖ Study scriptures on righteousness in the Gospels and Church Epistles using a biblical concordance to locate specific usages
- ❖ Review this chapter on **Oblivion of Righteousness** and meditate on its scriptures

27

OB #10: HOPE OBLIVION

*The spiritual oblivion of hope involves continually making decisions
that are motivated by the fear of death or by misconceptions
regarding life after death. Man is concerned with issues of death
MORE THAN or INSTEAD OF his eternal life and Christ's return.*

*Hope consciousness solution: Accept that we already have
eternal life and that we look forward to the hope of the return
of Christ MORE THAN OR INSTEAD OF maintaining false
hope, hopelessness, and/or a constant fear of death and dying.*

The outcome of this **oblivion of hope** is preparation for death and/or the
live-for-today belief that we are to "eat, drink and be merry, for tomorrow
we die." In some cases, this unreal sense of hope can lead to "spiritualism"
with the belief that one can talk to the dead. This **oblivion** can leave one
with feelings of depression and a chronic morbidity concerning the future.

*By his death and resurrection, Jesus Christ lifted our
consciousness from the mental bondage of fear of death.*

Hebrews 2:14-15:

Forasmuch then as the children are partakers of flesh
and blood, he [Jesus Christ] himself took part of the same;
that through death he might destroy him that had the
power of death, that is the devil;

And deliver them who through fear of death were all their lifetime subject to bondage.

Created in God's image (Spirit), we have eternal life and the hope of the return of Jesus Christ, which is called the "anchor of the soul." Looking forward to his return keeps us mentally stabilized.

Hebrews 6:19 (a):
Which hope we have as an anchor of the soul, both sure and stedfast.

Jesus is absolutely coming back. When he does, we will meet him in the air and forever be with him.

I Thessalonians 4:13-18:
But I would not have you to be ignorant [uninformed], brethren, concerning them which are asleep [no longer alive], that ye sorrow not, even as others [unbelievers in Christ] which have no hope [for the future].

For if we believe that Jesus died and rose again, even them also which sleep [are not alive] in Jesus will God bring with him.

For this we say unto you by the word of the Lord, that we which are alive and remain unto the coming of the Lord shall not prevent [come before] them which are asleep [Some believers will be alive when Christ returns; others will be asleep].

For the Lord himself shall descend from heaven with a shout, with the voice of the archangel, and with the trump [trumpet] of God: and the dead in Christ shall rise first:

Then we which are alive and remain shall be caught
up together with them in the clouds, to meet the Lord in
the air: and so shall we ever be with the Lord.

Wherefore comfort one another with these words.

Before we came to a consciousness of Christ, we were "without Christ,
being aliens from the commonwealth of Israel, and strangers from the
covenant of promise, having no hope, and without God in the world"
(Ephesians 2:12). The Apostle Paul stated emphatically that Jesus Christ
is our only hope now and in the future. He is THE HOPE.

> I Timothy 1:1:
> Paul, an apostle of Jesus Christ by the commandment
> of God our Saviour, and Lord Jesus Christ, which [who]
> is our hope.

If we place our hope in anyone or anything else, we are going to be very
disappointed. There are so many people who spend their lives preparing
for their retirement. Others are living for today without any sense of where
they are heading. Those who do not know or believe in their divine nature
delude themselves into believing that, as mortals, they will live forever.

In I Corinthians, chapter15, Paul provided evidence of the resurrection of
Jesus Christ and the reality that the believer in Christ also will be raised up.

> Verses 20-23:
> But now is Christ risen from the dead, and become
> the first fruits of them that sleep [are not alive].
> For since by man [Adam] came death, by man [Christ]
> came also the resurrection of the dead.
> For as in Adam all [eventually] die, even so in Christ
> shall all be made alive. But every man in his own order:

Christ the first fruits; afterward they that are Christ's at his coming.

In verses 25-26, Paul makes a startling statement about death.

> For he must reign, till he hath put all enemies under his feet.
> The last enemy that shall be destroyed is death.

In the **oblivion of hope**, mortal man ends up embracing death and spends time accepting and preparing for it. The primary reason why we remain in this **crisis** is that we lack the knowledge of, have forgotten, are confused about, or refuse to accept the Scriptures and the power of God regarding the resurrection of Christ and our inherent divine nature created by God. In this *state of oblivion,* profoundly haunting questions prevail such as: *Where am I going? Is that all there is? What is my purpose?*

Since God will ultimately handle all critical situations and injustices of life, we can be comforted in surrendering our resentments and grudges to this later judgment by Him.

> Romans 2:5-6:
> But after thy hardness and impenitent heart treasurest up unto thyself wrath against the day of wrath and revelation of the righteous judgment of God [**dikaiokrisia**];
> Who will render to every man according to his deeds.

The Greek word, **dikaiokrisia** (from its root word, **crisis**) means, "the righteous judgment of God" on judgment day. God wants us to relinquish our sense of revenge toward anyone.

> Romans 12:19:

Dearly beloved, avenge [revenge] not yourselves, but rather give place unto wrath: for it is written, Vengeance is mine; I will repay, saith the Lord.

God's judgment now and in the end is by one man, Jesus Christ.

Acts 17:31:

Because he [God] hath appointed a day, in the which he [God] will judge [*crisis*] the world in righteousness by that man [Jesus Christ] whom he [God] hath ordained; whereof he hath given assurance unto all men, in that he raised him [Jesus] from the dead.

In this day and time of grace, God is not doing the judging. This is an age of His grace and mercy. An individual who does not choose to come to the spiritual enlightenment of Christ continues to judge himself. He has mentally condemned himself and has chosen to remain in a *spiritual oblivion of condemnation*.

II Peter 2:9:

The Lord knoweth how to deliver the godly out of temptations, and to reserve the unjust [those who choose to remain in condemnation because they elect not to believe in Jesus Christ as Savior and Lord] unto the day of judgment [*crisis*] to be punished.

In the "day of judgment," mortal man unaware of his spiritual nature ends up punishing himself because he rejects Jesus Christ. He remains in a mental state of spiritual unworthiness and perceived separation from God.

The Apostle Paul reminds us that "the Lord is the righteous judge [*krite*]" who will give a spiritual "crown of righteousness" to those who love the appearing of Jesus Christ.

II Timothy 4:7-8:

I have fought a good fight, I have finished my course, I have kept the faith [I gave testimony of the faith of Jesus Christ].

Henceforth there is laid up for me a crown of righteousness, which the Lord, the righteous judge, shall give me at that day: and not to me only, but unto all them also that love his [Christ's] appearing.

Paul was passionately motivated by the hope of the return of Jesus Christ.

Philippians 3:13-15:

Brethren, I count not myself to have apprehended [I have not arrived at the finished line yet, because Jesus Christ has not returned as yet]; but this one thing I do, forgetting those things which are behind, and reaching forth unto those things which are before,

I press toward the mark for the prize of the high [upward] calling of God in Christ Jesus.

Let us therefore, as many as be perfect [mature], be thus minded [have this goal] and if any thing ye be otherwise minded [if there be any other goal], God shall reveal even this to you.

We spiritually recognize the value of living and making decisions in light of the hope of the return of Christ. We know where we are going. We are already there spiritually in Christ. Our heart's desire is for others to know that they too can become spiritually conscious of eternal life.

Hope consciousness solution: Accept that we already have eternal life and that we look forward to the hope of the return

of Christ MORE THAN OR INSTEAD OF maintaining false hope, hopelessness, and/or a constant fear of death and dying.

Hope consciousness strategies:

❖ Study and visualize the scriptures in this chapter concerning the return of Christ

❖ Correct errors in thinking or conversation regarding the meaning of death

❖ Share the Word of God concerning how to receive eternal life

❖ Pray that "the eyes of our understanding" would be enlightened regarding the hope

❖ Make valiant decisions based upon the return of Christ

28

OB #11: EXAMPLE/COMPARISON OBLIVION

The Oblivion of Example/Comparison is a chronic valuing of status, examples, and role models from the world MORE THAN OR INSTEAD OF God and His Son who is THE example and role model for all time. The outcome of this crisis often is jealousy and unhealthy competition.

Hope consciousness solution: Value Christ as THE example and role model for our lives MORE THAN OR INSTEAD OF the perceived status, roles, and positions of self and/or others in the world and in the Bible.

II Corinthians 10:12:

For we dare not make ourselves of the number, or compare ourselves with some that commend [lift up] themselves: but they measuring themselves by themselves, and comparing themselves among themselves, are not wise.

Within the Body of Christ, every role or function is of equal importance to God. There are no insignificant jobs or big *honchos* within the One Body.

I Corinthians 12:18:

But now hath God set the members every one of them in the body, as it hath pleased him.

I Peter 2:21:

For even hereunto were ye called: because Christ also suffered for us, leaving us an example, that ye should follow in his steps.

To greatly value the example of Christ is to see all other well-known believers in the Old Testament (i.e., Moses, Joseph, David) as forerunners of Jesus Christ. He is "the beginner and finisher of our faith" (Hebrews 12:2). All of the law and the prophets bore witness to the coming of Christ and the righteousness of God, which is by the faith of Jesus Christ.

Acts 10:42-43:

And he [Christ] commanded us to preach unto the people, and to testify that it is he which was ordained of God to be the judge [*krite*] of the quick [the living] and the dead.

To him give all the prophets witness, that through his name whosoever believeth in him shall receive remission of sins.

Romans 3:21-22:

But now the righteousness of God without the law is manifested, being witnessed by the law and the prophets,

Even the righteousness of God which is by faith of Jesus Christ unto all and upon all them that believe: for there is no difference.

The entire Bible from Genesis to Revelation is the story of God (Spirit), His Son, and His Word. Old Testament believers and prophets looked to the coming of the Messiah who is our savior and Lord, Jesus Christ. Nothing and no one can compare with him and all that he accomplished. He is still doing amazing feats today as the "intercessor" that helps us to return to fellowship with the Father.

Romans 8:34:
Who is he that condemneth? It is Christ that died, yea rather, that is risen again, who is even at the right hand of God, who also maketh intercession for us.

The Christ is our life and true identity.

Colossians 3:3-4:
For ye are dead, and your life is hid with Christ in God.
When Christ, who is our life, shall appear, then shall ye also appear with him in glory.

The oblivion of example/comparison continues when we compare ourselves to others more than Christ and his unswerving obedience to God. The Scriptures strongly encourage us to lead every thought, judgment, or comparison captive to the Word of God.

II Corinthians 10:5:
Casting down imaginations [false reasoning] and every high [proud] thing that exalteth itself against the knowledge of God, and bringing into captivity every thought to the obedience of Christ.

I Corinthians 4:2-5 reminds us not to judge or criticize others or ourselves. We are not to value others' opinions or criticisms above what God thinks of us.

Moreover, it is required in stewards that a man be found faithful.

But with me it is a very small thing that I should be judged of you, or of man's judgment: yea, I judge not mine own self.

For I know nothing by myself; yet am I not hereby justified; but he that judgeth me is the Lord.

Therefore judge nothing before the time, until the Lord come, who both will bring to light the hidden things of darkness, and will make manifest the counsels of the hearts: and then shall every man have praise of God.

We are not to judge one another "any more."

Romans 14:10, 13:

But why dost thou judge thy brother? or why does thou set at nought [reduce to nothing; devalue] thy brother? for we shall all stand before the judgment seat of Christ.

Let us not therefore judge one another any more; but judge this rather, that no man put a stumbling block or an occasion to fall in his brother's way.

When we stand before the "judgment seat" at Christ's return, we will not be judged negatively or be punished because we have already been judged in Christ and have been found innocent. Today, the Word of God does the judging and valuing.

Hebrews 4:12:

For the Word of God is quick, and powerful, and sharper than any two-edged sword, piercing even to the dividing asunder of soul and spirit, and of the joints and marrow, and is a discerner [a critic; the standard] of the thoughts and intents of the heart.

Colossians 2:16:

Let no man therefore judge you in meat [food], or drink, or in respect of an holy day, or of the new moon, or of the sabbath days.

The oblivion of example/comparison will dissipate if we consistently give greater value to our divine nature and identity in Christ. We look to Christ as the head of the body of believers and the center of our lives.

Colossians 2:19:

And not holding the Head, from which all the body [the One Body of Christ] by joints and bands having nourishment ministered, and knit together, increaseth with the increase of God.

Example/comparison consciousness solution: Value Christ as THE example and role model for our lives MORE THAN OR INSTEAD OF the perceived status, roles, and positions of self and/or others in the world and in the Bible.

Example/comparison successful consciousness strategies:

❖ Study the life, death and resurrection of Christ to appreciate His example
❖ See others' needs and presses through the loving eyes of Jesus Christ
❖ Ask: *God, what should I do in this circumstance? What would Jesus do in a specific conflicting situation?* Then, expect to receive an answer.

❖ Avoid comparisons to others
❖ Do not judge others. Only God and His Word do the judging
❖ Equally respect the value, work and function of all men
❖ Appreciate your divine nature and stay humble in comparison to others
❖ Review and meditate upon the scriptures in this chapter on *Hope Oblivion.*

Part VI: Summary: Worship Oblivion

One Major Oblivion:

I. Worship Oblivion: (1) lack of spiritual consciousness of the One true all-loving God, (2) spiritual misunderstanding of the accuracy of the Word, and (3) spiritual unawareness of man's inherent worth and divine nature created in God's image (Spirit).

Spiritual Oblivion: Subtypes of Oblivion (C.C.H.I.I.L.D.R.R.E.N.)

C = Condemnation of self and others; maintaining a deep sense of sin-consciousness and mental unworthiness MORE THAN or INSTEAD OF the spiritual unawareness that we are created in God's image and are spiritual beings

C = Conversations that consistently value communication with the world MORE THAN or INSTEAD OF fellowship with God through prayer, the Scriptures, and conversations with other likeminded believers

H = Hope from the world MORE THAN or INSTEAD OF hope in God through Christ

I = Integrity and lies of the world are believed MORE THAN or INSTEAD OF the spiritual accuracy of the Word of God and what is says about worship and our worthiness

I = Incongruence between study and practice of the Word of God because of five-sense worldly distractions MORE THAN or INSTEAD OF a

spiritual sense and taking valiant action on the
full gospel of Christ

L = Love of self and the world MORE THAN or
INSTEAD OF the love of God in Christ

D = Discerning by five sense analysis MORE THAN
or INSTEAD OF spiritual discernment from God

R = Righteousness by self-works, arrogance and pride
MORE THAN or INSTEAD OF the righteousness
of God

R = Research by accepting the world's intellectual
view of the Bible with its private and religious
interpretation MORE THAN OR INSTEAD OF
carefully evaluating the spiritual accuracy of the
Word

E = Example/comparison from the world MORE
THAN or INSTEAD OF accepting the ultimate
example of Christ

N = Need/sufficiency supplied by oneself or others
MORE THAN or INSTEAD OF sufficiency from
God through Christ

Mortal man with spiritual oblivion may have one or more of the these
types that may or may not be experienced or manifested in the natural
world. In addition, man may have one or more of the subtypes at any
one time or at different times. These varieties are not presumed to be
an exhaustive list but a starting point for biblical consideration and
research. These spiritual subtypes can trigger personal and worldly

crises or they can be the consequence of internal and/or external natural critical conditions. There is no order to these subtypes, and no subtype is more significant than another.

Worldly orientations are vastly different from spiritual intervention. In this spiritual intervention, the goal is to encourage not only intellectual self-awareness but, more significantly, spiritual consciousness of love, namely, our love toward and from God. As we grow in the grace of loving God, through worship, respect for His Word, and an appreciation of our divine worth, we will love ourselves as God loves us, and ultimately love others, as God in Christ loved us.

PART VII
FROM OBLIVION TO CONSCIOUSNESS

The only antidote for spiritual oblivion is gracious growth in spiritual grace and consciousness concerning true worship, understanding of the Word, and acceptance of man's inherent divine worthiness. When an individual places his greatest weight on spiritual values concerning God through an uplifting and enlightening knowledge of Christ, he has shifted away from oblivion to spiritual consciousness.

Philippians 2:12-14 describes deliverance from oblivion through *spiritual consciousness intervention*.

> Wherefore, my beloved, as ye have always obeyed, not as in my presence only, but now much more in my absence, work out your own salvation [the wholeness and completeness you already have] with fear and trembling [respect and awe].
>
> For it is God which worketh in you [by way of the Spirit and the Scriptures] both to will and to do of His good pleasure.
>
> Do all things [manifest your spiritual valueness by doing valuable things] without murmurings and disputings.

In contrast to worldly standards of human awareness, *consciousness intervention* began by God after man lost a sense of spiritual consciousness of his divine nature. God sent His Son, Jesus Christ, to redeem mankind from the ***oblivion of the true worship of God, the true Word and one's inherent true worth***. He lifted man's spiritual consciousness from condemnation and sin-consciousness to the truth of worship, the Word and his spiritual worth. On the day of Pentecost, "The Comforter" (Holy Spirit) provided greater spiritual enlightenment of God's truth, love and power. The grace of spiritual consciousness is available to anyone who hungers to know and relate to God and His Son intimately. The spiritual reality of truly confessing Jesus as Lord and believing that God raised him from the dead continues to elevate man's spiritual awareness.

> Romans10: 9:
> That if thou shalt confess with thy mouth the Lord
> Jesus, and shalt believe in thine heart that God hath raised
> him from the dead, thou shalt be saved [made whole].

Any critical situation that we experience in this lifetime is light compared to the eternal glory of being with Christ forever at his coming and the reality that we already have eternal life here and now.

> I Cor. 4:17:
> For our light affliction which is but for a moment
> worketh for us a far more exceeding and eternal weight
> [value] of glory.

Because God works in us by way of the Holy Spirit, we are able to work out (exercise our mental and spiritual muscles) regarding who we worship, what the Word says we have in Christ, and what purpose we have as spiritual beings. This "renewed mind" (Romans 12:2) regimen involves continuous bombardments of spiritual understanding of God and His Word. Through a deepening sense of the Word, we learn to change our focus to spiritual matters more than the temporal things of this world.

II Corinthians 4:18:

> While we look not at the things which are seen [things of the world; pressures facing us], but at the things which are not seen [the Word of God]: for the things which are seen are temporal; but the things which are not seen are eternal.

Whenever difficult situations arise in life, God makes it available for us to turn to Him for inspiration through prayer and His Word.

Steps to Maintaining and Reclaiming Spiritual Consciousness:

- ❖ *Accept the spiritual reality of our inherent spiritual consciousness*
- ❖ *Identify the specific type of spiritual oblivion (Questionnaire, Parts I, II)*
- ❖ *Study the Scriptures in the chapters of this book on specific subtype(s)*
- ❖ *Explore errors in thinking about the meaning of the Scriptures in the chapter*
- ❖ *Develop intervention/goals for specific types of oblivion (Checklist, Parts 1, II)*
- ❖ *Employ "spiritual valorization" to evaluate errors in thinking and false mental patterns concerning spiritual values of worship and their corresponding scriptures*
- ❖ *Pursue spiritual valorization to evaluate uplifting Christ-centered verses on spiritual identity*

29

STEP ONE: ACCEPT OUR INHERENT SPIRITUAL CONSCIOUSNESS

Spiritual consciousness began with and by God. Spiritual consciousness is a deeper awareness of the meaning of true worship: "We worship God in Spirit and in truth (John 4:4)." This consciousness involves a spiritual understanding of the omnipotence of God, the one true God, through inspired prayer, the operation of "the nine manifestations of the Spirit" (I Cor. 12), and continued spiritual understanding of the written Word of God, His spoken Word and the Word "in the flesh" (Jesus Christ). This is the spiritual meaning of true spiritual worship.

Consciousness Level #1: The spiritual awareness that "God is Spirit" (John 4:4) and that we are created in His image, which is Spirit.

Spiritual consciousness is a continued moment-by-moment, here and now awakening to the true spiritual reality that all men and women are created in God's image, which is Spirit (Genesis 1:26-27). We have an eternal spiritual relationship with God that can never be lost or replaced. WE ARE SPIRITUAL AND ALWAYS WILL BE SPIRITUAL BEINGS. This fundamental and primary level of awareness ultimately replaces long-held mortal awareness of sin-consciousness and self-consciousness.

Consciousness Level #2: A spiritual understanding that Jesus Christ brought us to a new level of love, truth and grace by his life, death, resurrection and the ascension.

Grace came with Jesus Christ. By his crucifixion and resurrection, he exhibited, enlightened and enlarged our consciousness to the power of Spirit over matter, the power of spiritual consciousness over mortal beliefs and thoughts. He overcame our false sense of sin-consciousness, unworthiness and self-consciousness. *In level 2, we spiritually come to understand and become aware of the Christ Spirit that was in Christ and now and always has been our divine spiritual nature as God's spiritual beings created in His image.* Through Jesus Christ, we gained a full level of man's true God-given consciousness.

Consciousness Level #3: Knowing, believing and manifesting God's spiritual love (I Cor. 13).

We have a spiritual awakening to the meaning of God's love and how to manifest it as true spiritual beings to others.

Consciousness Level #4: Operate the nine "manifestations of the Holy Spirit."

> I Corinthians 12:7-11:
> But the manifestation of the Spirit is given to every man to profit withal.
> 8 For to one is given by the Spirit the word of wisdom; to another the word of knowledge by the same Spirit;
> 9 To another faith by the same Spirit; to another the gifts of healing by the same Spirit;
> 10 To another the working of miracles; to another prophecy; to another discerning of spirits; to another *divers* kinds of tongues; to another the interpretation of tongues:
> 11 But all these worketh that one and the selfsame Spirit, dividing to every man severally as he will.

Consciousness Level #5:
Spiritually "renew our minds" to God's values and Word so that we
maintain a "spiritual mindset" toward Him.

> I Corinthians 2:16(b):
> But we have the mind of Christ.

There is an ongoing "renewing of the mind" to spiritual truth about God, Christ, Holy Spirit and the reality of our spiritual being. It is a negation of the reality and power of a materialistic world that has no likeness to Spirit.

> Romans 12:8:
> And be not conformed to this world (matter and materialism) but be ye transformed by the renewing of your mind.

Our spiritual mindset is a mind that is already designed for the purpose of receiving, retaining and releasing the true and accurate Word of God. It accepts truth and exposes errors in thinking. It is comparable to a template for the Word. We are to "lead every thought captive to the Word."

30

STEP TWO: IDENTIFY OBLIVION SUBTYPES

USING QUESTIONNAIRE, PART I, IDENTIFY SPECIFIC SPIRITUAL SUBTYPES OF OBLIVION OF WORSHIP (SEE BELOW). WE MAY HAVE ONE OR MORE OF THE SUBTYPES AT ANY ONE TIME OR AT DIFFERENT TIMES.

IN QUESTIONNAIRE, PART II, EXPLORE THE NATURE OF EACH SUBTYPE, AND HOW AND WHY WE CONSISTENTLY LACK SPIRITUAL CONSCIOUSNESS OF TRUTH IN THESE AREAS.

Questionnaire: Part I
Subtypes of Oblivion

Below are subtypes of worship oblivion. Each represents one area of life in which the individual values self or the world more than Christ. A person or group may have one or more of these subtypes concurrently.

*Circle the specific type(s) that apply to your specific condition or situation.

Subtypes of Worship Oblivion

(C.C.H.I.I.L.D.R.E.N.)

C= Condemnation oblivion: Valuing thought patterns of sin-consciousness and mental unworthiness MORE THAN or INSTEAD OF pursuing spiritual consciousness that man is a spiritual being created in God's image

C = Conversation oblivion: Valuing conversations with self/others MORE THAN or INSTEAD OF God through Christ

H = Hope oblivion: Valuing hopelessness and death MORE THAN or INSTEAD OF hope in the return of Christ Jesus

I = Integrity oblivion: Valuing facts and lies of the world MORE THAN or INSTEAD OF the truth of the Word of God concerning Christ

I = Incongruence oblivion: Valuing an intellectual or superficial understanding of parts of God's magnified Word MORE THAN or INSTEAD OF graciously seeking spiritual consciousness of the Word

L = Love oblivion: Valuing love from self or the world MORE THAN or INSTEAD OF the love of God and His Son

D =Discerning oblivion: Valuing the analysis of situations by the five senses MORE THAN or INSTEAD OF discerning spiritual information

R = Righteousness oblivion: Valuing self-righteousness, ego and pride from the world MORE THAN or INSTEAD OF accepting the righteousness Of God in Christ

E =Example/comparison oblivion: Valuing examples or comparisons from the world MORE THAN or INSTEAD OF comparisons from the Bible

N =Need/sufficiency oblivion: Valuing self-need and self-sufficiency in relation to the world MORE THAN or INSTEAD OF the abundance, grace, and sufficiency of God

Questionnaire: Part II

Describe your current situation in light of oblivion subtypes you have chosen:

I.   *Worship Oblivion:*

Love Oblivion
The individual values a fake deceitful love of the world or hypocritical love toward God, self, and others MORE THAN the true love of God.

Describe:

Need/sufficiency Oblivion
The individual values his own or the world's sufficiency MORE THAN God's sufficiency in all things.

Describe:

Discerning Oblivion

He/she values a five-senses approach to analyzing circumstances and events MORE THAN a spiritual and biblical viewpoint regarding people, places, and things.

Describe:

II. *Worship and the Word of God Oblivion:*

Conversation Oblivion

He/she values conversations, wisdom, and help from some other ungodly and distorted worldly sources MORE THAN spiritual dialogue with God through the Scriptures, faithful believers, and godly trainers.

Describe:

Incongruence Oblivion

He/she values worldly distractions and intellectual interpretations of the Bible MORE THAN spiritual consciousness of God and the full Gospel of Christ.

Describe:

Integrity Oblivion

He/she values facts, lies or some other standards from the world MORE THAN the integrity and accuracy of the Word of God as the primary standard for living.

Describe:

III. *Worship and Spiritual Worth Oblivion:*

Example/comparison Oblivion

He/she values the status, fame and models from the world MORE THAN the example of Christ and other believers in the Bible.

Describe:

Hope Oblivion

He/she values chance future events and preparation for death MORE THAN the future with God, eternal life, and the hope of the return of Jesus Christ.

Describe:

Righteousness Oblivion

The troubled individual values, spends more time, gives more attention to, invests more in his old behavior patterns and a sense of condemnation or self-righteousness MORE THAN his righteousness in Christ.

Describe:

Condemnation Oblivion

The individual values and accepts continued inherent guilt, sin-consciousness and mental condemnation MORE Than his Divine nature and the reality that he is created in God's image (spirit).

Describe:

LIST THE PEOPLE, PLACES, AND THINGS THAT YOU VALUE

31

STEP THREE: DEVELOP SPIRITUALLY CONSCIOUS GOALS

Decide and evaluate consciousness goals for a specific situation so that you can maintain right thinking regarding worship, the Word, and our worth specific to our particular level and circumstance.

USE CONSCIOUSNESS GOALS CHECKLIST, PARTS I AND II.

Checklist, Part I:

Spiritually Conscious Goals

Note: The Consciousness Goals (below) are Opposite the Worship Oblivion Types.

*Place a check next to the desired goals

Worship Goals:

_____*Love consciousness goal* = craving the Love of God MORE THAN OR INSTEAD OF the love of the world

_____*Discerning consciousness goal* = pursuing spiritual discernment from God MORE THAN OR INSTEAD OF five sense worldly analyses

_____*Need/sufficiency consciousness goal* = accepting sufficiency from God through Christ MORE THAN OR INSTEAD OF need/sufficiency from oneself or others

Worship through the Word Goals:

_____*Integrity consciousness goal* = valuing and researching the integrity, accuracy, spiritual understanding of the Word of God MORE THAN OR INSTEAD OF the lies of the world

_____*Incongruence consciousness goal* = seeking spiritual consciousness concerning the full Gospel of Christ MORE THAN OR INSTEAD OF a partial and imbalanced understanding of the Word of God

_____*Conversation consciousness goal* = fellowshipping with God through prayer and the Word MORE THAN OR INSTEAD OF conversations with oneself or others

Worship through Consciousness of Worth:

__*Condemnation consciousness goal* = accepting that man is a spiritual being created in God's image MORE THAN OR INSTEAD OF mental condemnation

_____*Hope consciousness goal* = hope in God through Christ MORE THAN OR INSTEAD OF hope from the world

_____*Righteousness consciousness goal* = seeking the righteousness of God MORE THAN OR INSTEAD OF righteousness by self-works

_____*Example/comparison consciousness goal* = following THE example of Christ MORE THAN OR INSTEAD examples and comparison from the world

` *Checklist- Part II:*

Course for Resolving Subtypes of Oblivion

Prioritize consciousness goals and affirmations related to physical, emotional and/or interpersonal conditions.

Explain your specific course for resolving the oblivion:

_____Instead of the ***oblivion of righteousness***, I desire to spiritually grow in the comprehension and conviction that CHRIST-IS RIGHTEOUSNESS (Romans 3:21-25), THEREFORE, AS A SPIRITUAL BEING IN CHRIST, I AM RIGHTEOUS.

Explain: _____

_____Instead of the ***oblivion of love***, I desire to spiritually grow in the comprehension and conviction that GOD IS LOVE AND CHRIST-IS LOVE (Ephesians 5:2). THEREFORE, AS A SPIRITUAL MAN, I AM LOVED AND LOVABLE.

Explain: _____

_____Instead of the ***oblivion of hope***, I desire to spiritually grow in the comprehension and conviction that CHRIST-IS OUR HOPE (I Tim. 1:1), and that it is "CHRIST IN ME, THE HOPE OF GLORY" (Col. 1:27).

Explain: _____

_____Instead of the *oblivion of integrity* concerning the Bible, I desire to spiritually grow in the comprehension of and conviction to the FULL GOSPEL OF CHRIST, WHO IS THE LIVING WORD.

Explain: _____

_____Instead of the *oblivion of need/sufficiency*, I desire to spiritually grow in the comprehension and conviction that GOD IS MY SUFFICIENCY (II Cor. 3:4-6). THERFORE, I HAVE ALL SUFFICIENCY IN ALL THINGS.

Explain: _____

_____Instead of the *oblivion of example/comparison*, I desire to spiritually grow in the comprehension and conviction that CHRIST-IS MY EXAMPLE (Hebrews 12: 1-3).

Explain: _____

_____Instead of the *oblivion of conversation*, I desire to spiritually grow in the comprehension of and conviction to THE MOVEMENT OF THE WORD OF GOD, AND TO PREACH IN SEASON AND OUT OF SEASON (Eph. 2:18; II Tim. 4:2).

Explain: _____

_____Instead of the oblivion *of discerning*, I desire to spiritually grow in the comprehension and conviction that GOD WORKS IN ME BY WAY OF THE HOLY SPIRIT. "THE LORD IS THAT SPIRIT" (II Cor. 3:18).

Explain: _____

_____Instead of the *oblivion of incongruence*, I desire to grow IN UNDERSTANDING AND PRACTICE OF THE SPIRITUAL SENSE OF THE WORD (II Timothy 2:15-16)

Explain: _____

_____Instead of the *oblivion of condemnation*, I seek increased spiritual consciousness of MY DIVINE NATURE CREATED IN THE IMAGE OF GOD (GEN. 1:26-27)

Explain: _____

32

STEP FOUR: EVALUATE VALUES OF WORSHIP

Using the spiritual valorization process of doctrine/reproof/correction:

a. *Evaluate the "values of worship" and their relationship to the subtype of oblivion.*

b. *Discuss what these values convey for your situation and your ideas on worship.*

c. *Consider and meditate upon each spiritual value and the specific scriptures provided.*

d. *Ask the following strategic questions regarding doctrine/ reproof/correction of each of the "spiritual values":*

*Doctrine = Valuate each verse:
Do I value or appreciate the verse?
Do I understand the verse, and the verse in context of the chapter?
What does the verse mean spiritually?

*Reproof = E-valuate the verse:
What are my errors in thinking regarding this in the verse?
Do I agree with the idea of the verse?
Is my life a reflection or contradiction of this verse?

*Correction = RE-valuate the verse:
How can I bring my life back to right thinking of the verse?
How do I compare my current concerns with this verse?
How do I make things right in my life so that they agree with what the Word says about my worth and divine nature?

The following SPIRITUAL VALUES encompass true worship:

1. Supremely value (worship) God, the Father of Jesus Christ

John 4:23-24: But the hour cometh, and now is, when the true worshippers shall worship the Father in spirit and in truth: for the Father seeketh such to worship him. God is a Spirit: and they that worship him must worship him in spirit and in truth.

2. Value Jesus Christ, God's only begotten Son

John 10:10-11:The thief cometh not, but for to steal, and to kill, and to destroy: I am come that they might have life, and that they might have it more abundantly.

John 5:22-23: For the Father judgeth no man, but hath committed all judgment unto the Son: that all men should honor the Son, even as they honor the Father. He that honoreth not the Son honoreth not the Father which hath sent him.

3. Value a spiritual understanding of the accurate Word of God

John 1:1: In the beginning was the Word, and the Word was with God, and the Word was God. The same was in the beginning with God.

II Timothy 2:15: Study to show thyself approved unto God, a workman that needeth not to be ashamed, rightly dividing the word of truth.

II Timothy 3:16-17: All Scripture is given by inspiration of God, and is profitable for doctrine, for reproof, for correction, for instruction in righteousness: that the man of God may be perfect, thoroughly furnished unto all good works.

John 8:31-32: Then said Jesus to those Jews which believed on him, If ye continue in my word, then are ye my disciples indeed; and ye shall know the truth, and the truth shall make you free.

4. Value the work of "The Comforter" (Holy Spirit)

I Corinthians 2:11-12: For what man knoweth the things of a man, save the spirit of man which is in him? even so the things of God knoweth no man, but the Spirit of God. Now we have received, not the spirit of the world, but the Spirit which is of God; that we might know the things that are freely given to us of God.

John 15:26: But when the Comforter is come, whom I will send unto you from the Father, even the Spirit of truth, which proceedeth from the Father, he shall testify of me:

II Timothy 1:7: For God hath not given us the spirit of fear; but of power, and of love, and of a sound mind.

5. Value "godliness" (an ongoing relationship with God through prayer)

I Timothy 4:8: For bodily exercise profiteth little: but godliness is profitable unto all things, having promise of the life that now is, and of that which is to come.

I Timothy 6:3-7: If any man teach otherwise, and consent not to wholesome words, even the words of our Lord Jesus Christ, and to the doctrine which is according to godliness; he is proud, knowing nothing, but doting about questions and strifes of words, whereof cometh envy, strife, railings, evil surmisings, perverse disputings of men of corrupt minds, and destitute of the truth, supposing that gain is godliness: from such withdraw thyself. But godliness with contentment is great gain. For we brought nothing into this world, and it is certain we can carry nothing out.

6. **Value the "one spiritual body of Christ"**

I Corinthians 12:12-13: For as the body is one, and hath many members and all the members of that one body, being many, are one body: so also is Christ. For by one Spirit are we all baptized into one body, whether we be Jews or Gentiles, whether we be bond or free; and have been all made to drink into one Spirit.

7. **Value all men for Christ, since we are all created in God's image (Spirit)**

Genesis 1:26-27: And God said, Let us make man in our image, after our likeness: and let them have dominion over the fish of the sea, and over the fowl of the air, and over the cattle, and over all the earth, and over every creeping thing that creepeth upon the earth. So God created man in his *own* image, in the image of God created he him; male and female created he them.

8. **Value man's inherent divine nature and identity**

Ephesians 2:10: For we are his workmanship, created in Christ Jesus unto good works, which God hath before ordained that we should walk in them.

II Peter 1:3-4: According as his divine power hath given unto us all things that *pertain* unto life and godliness, through the knowledge of him that hath called us to glory and virtue: whereby are given unto us exceeding great and precious promises; that by these ye might be partakers of the divine nature, having escaped the corruption that is in the world through lust.

9. Value the love of God

Matthew 22:37-39: Jesus said unto him, THOU SHALT LOVE THE LORD THY GOD WITH ALL THY HEART, AND WITH ALL THY SOUL, AND WITH ALL THY MIND. This is the first and great [most valued] commandment. And the second is like unto it: thou shalt love thy neighbor as thyself.

Romans 8:38-39: For I am persuaded, that neither death, nor life, nor angels, nor principalities, nor powers, nor things present, nor things to come, nor height, nor depth, nor any other creature, shall be able to separate us from the love of God, which is in Christ Jesus our Lord.

10. Value the wisdom of God

Prov.1:2-4: To know wisdom and instruction; to perceive the words of understanding; to receive the instruction of wisdom, justice, and judgment, and equity; to give subtilty to the simple, to the young man knowledge and discretion.

Ephesians 1:17-18: that the God of our Lord Jesus Christ, the Father of glory, may give unto you the spirit of wisdom and revelation in the knowledge of him: the eyes of your understanding being enlightened; that ye may know what is the hope of his calling, and what the riches of the glory of his inheritance in the saints,

I Corinthians 1:30-31: But of him are ye in Christ Jesus, who of God is made unto us wisdom, and righteousness, and sanctification, and redemption: that, according as it is written, He that glorieth, let him glory in the Lord.

Synopsis: To worship or supremely value God, the Father of Jesus Christ, is our first and foremost purpose. Toward this goal, we pursue all other spiritual values. We worship or supremely value God BY valuing His Son, His Word and the Holy Spirit, our worth as spiritual beings, our ongoing relationship with Him through prayer ("godliness"), His children ("the One Body of Christ"), and His love and wisdom. Our lifelong excursion into these spiritual qualities will enable us to capture the one and only true spiritual consciousness.

33

STEP FIVE: USE THE PRINCIPLE OF SPIRITUAL VALORIZATION

Spiritual valorization involves the harmonious spiritual process of doctrine, reproof, and correction.

II Timothy 3:16:

All scripture [from Genesis to Revelation] is given by inspiration of God and is profitable [valuable] for *doctrine* [what to value], for *reproof* [where we are off balance in our values], for *correction* [how to correct our errors and return to right values], for [which is] instruction in righteousness [how to live out this spiritually valued life for God].

The Apostle Paul discussed the importance of doctrine, reproof, and correction in accurately studying the Bible and understanding its spiritual meaning.

<u>Doctrine</u>

Doctrine is right thinking regarding the accuracy of the Word. The individual endeavors to study and rightly divide and spiritually understand the Word of God.

II Timothy 2:15-16:

Study to shew thyself approved unto God [Give time and energy to the Scriptures so as to prove to yourself that you have already been accepted and made valued], a workman that needeth not to be ashamed [need not be confounded as to who you are in Christ], rightly dividing the Word of truth [carefully researching the Scriptures as they relate to Jesus Christ, who is "the living Word of God"].

But shun profane and vain babblings: for they will increase unto ungodliness.

Reproof

Reproof involves evaluating, estimating, and/or weighing the Scriptures. We compare, contrast, and synchronize the Word with current issues, problems, and presses. We continue to examine our errors in thinking regarding the world and attempt to lead every thought back to Christ and the Word.

II Corinthians 10:5:

Casting down imaginations, and every high [false] thing that exalteth itself against the knowledge of God, and bringing into captivity every thought to the obedience of Christ.

The Apostle Paul exhorted believers to evaluate their beliefs in light of the Word of Christ and to be constantly reminded that Christ is in them.

II Corinthians 13:5:

Examine [evaluate] yourselves whether ye be in the faith [whether your thoughts and values are in line with the Word of God concerning Christ]; prove your own selves [continually evaluate and re-prove to yourselves that you are what the Word of God says you are in Christ]. Know ye not your own selves [Don't you know your valueness in Christ], how that Jesus Christ is in you, except ye be reprobates [except it be that your minds are out of touch with the Scriptures and the work of Christ]?

Sometimes, reproof connotes harshness toward or displeasure with a person's thinking. In reality, it is a loving process of allowing an individual to hear the soundness of the Word of God regarding a specific issue. Through the Scriptures and the Holy Spirit, the person himself is reproved. The Holy Spirit "proves again" to him how valuable he is.

Correction

Correction of the Word involves a return to right thinking about the Word. It is the valorization process of re-valuing or reviewing the importance and truth of the Word. Challenging discussions and debates personally with God or with others involve the serious discrepancies between the Word of God and the individual's continued deception and denials.

In II Corinthians 13:10, Paul stated:

Therefore, I write these things being absent, lest being present I should use sharpness [correction], according to the power which the Lord hath given me to edification, and not to destruction.

Through the valorization process of doctrine, reproof, and correction, we shift our thoughts and beliefs from the world to Christ.

34

STEP SIX: EVALUATE CHRIST-CENTERED VERSES ON SPIRITUAL WORTH

Using the spiritual valorization process of doctrine/reproof/correction:

a. *Evaluate the following uplifting Christ-centered scriptures (See below) that highlight your divine nature and spiritual worth*

b. *Discuss, meditate upon and verbalize each scripture to increase your basic understanding of its spiritual meaning.*

c. *Ask the following strategic questions regarding doctrine/ reproof/correction of "Christ-centered verses on spiritual identity":*

*Doctrine = Valuate each verse:
Do I value or appreciate the verse?
Do I understand the verse, and the verse in context of the chapter?
What does the verse mean spiritually?

*Reproof = E-valuate the verse:
What are my errors in thinking regarding this in the verse?
Do I agree with the idea of the verse?
Is my life a reflection or contradiction of this verse?

*Correction = Re-valuate the verse:
How can I bring my life back to right thinking of the verse?
How do I compare my present situation *with this verse?*

How do I make things right in my life so that they agree with what the Word says about my true and inherent spiritual worth?

<u>*Christ-centered Verses on Spiritual Identity:*</u>

No Condemnation in Christ: "There is therefore now no condemnation to them which are in Christ Jesus, who walk not after the flesh, but after the Spirit (Romans 8:1)."

Healed in Christ: "If [Since] the Spirit of him that raised up Jesus from the dead dwell in you, he [God] that raised up Christ from the dead shall also quicken [make alive] your mortal bodies by his Spirit that dwelleth in you (Romans 8:11)."

Victory in Christ: "...in all these things we are more than conquerors through him that loved us (Romans 8:37)."

Love of Christ: "For I am persuaded, that neither death, nor life, nor angels, nor principalities, nor powers, nor things present, nor things to come, nor height, nor depth, nor any creature, shall be able to separate us from the love of God, which is in Christ Jesus our Lord (Romans 8:38-39)."

Saved in Christ: "That if thou shalt confess with thy mouth the Lord Jesus, and shalt believe in thine heart that God hath raised him from the dead, thou shalt be saved [made whole] (Romans 10:9)."

Rights in Christ: "But of him are ye in Christ Jesus who of God is made unto us wisdom, and righteousness, and sanctification, and redemption (I Cor. 1:30)."

The Mind of Christ: "...but we have the mind of Christ [spiritually] (I Cor. 2:16(b))."

Promises in Christ: "For all the promises of God in him [Jesus Christ] are yea, and in him Amen, unto the glory of God by us (II Cor. 1:20)."

Sufficiency through Christ: "And such trust have we through Christ to God-ward: Not that we are sufficient of ourselves to think anything as of ourselves; but our sufficiency is of God; who also hath made us able ministers of the new testament (II Cor. 3:4-6(a))."

"And God is able to make all grace abound toward you; that ye, always having all sufficiency in all things, may abound to every good work (II Cor. 9:8)."

Triumph in Christ: "Now thanks be unto God, which always causeth us to triumph in Christ, and maketh manifest the savour of his knowledge by us in every place (II Cor. 2:14)."

Newness in Christ: "Therefore if any man be in Christ, he is a new creature: old things are passed away; behold, all things are become new (II Cor. 5:17)."

Faith of Christ: "I am crucified with Christ: nevertheless I live; yet not I, but Christ liveth in me: and the life which I now live in the flesh I live by the faith of the Son of God, who loved me, and gave himself for me (Gal. 2:20)."

Redeemed in Christ: "Christ hath redeemed us from the curse of the law, being made a curse for us (Gal. 3:13(a))."

All spiritual blessings in Christ: "Blessed be the God and Father of our Lord Jesus Christ, who hath blessed us with all spiritual blessings in heavenly places in Christ (Eph. 1:3)."

Masterpiece in Christ: "For we are his workmanship [masterpiece] created in Christ Jesus unto good works, which God hath before ordained that we should walk in them (Eph. 2:10)."

Access through Christ: "For through him [Christ] we both have access by one Spirit unto the Father (Eph. 2:18)."

Power in Christ: "Now unto him that is able to do exceeding abundantly above all that we ask or think, according to the power that worketh in us, unto him be glory in the church by Christ Jesus throughout all ages, world without end. Amen (Eph. 3:20-21)."

God works in us: "For it is God which worketh in you both to will and to do of his good pleasure (Phil. 2:13)."

Strength in Christ: "I can do all things through Christ which strengtheneth me (Phil. 4:13)."

Christ in you: "To whom God would make known what is the riches of the glory of this mystery among the Gentiles; which is Christ in you, the hope of glory (Col. 1:27)."

Complete in Christ: "And ye are complete in him [Christ], which is the head of all principality and power (Col. 2:10)."

ALERT: Look at your new divine nature by consistently studying the seven Church Epistles that will uplift and free you from obsessing on putrid thoughts. By consistently studying the word concerning the Lord Christ Jesus and walking by the Spirit of God, you will automatically starve the lusts of the flesh (all aspects of materialism).

Romans 13:14:

But put on the Lord Jesus Christ, and make not provision for the flesh, to fulfil the lusts thereof."

Summary, Part VII

Pursue the Following Steps to Gain or Reclaim Spiritual Consciousness:

- ❖ *Accept the reality that we have inherent spiritual consciousness*
- ❖ *Identify the specific type of spiritual oblivion (Questionnaire, Parts I, II)*
- ❖ *Study the Scriptures in the chapters of this book on specific subtype(s)*
- ❖ *Explore errors in thinking about the meaning of the Scriptures in the chapter*
- ❖ *Develop intervention/goals for specific types of oblivion (Checklist, Parts 1, II)*
- ❖ *Employ "SPIRITUAL VALORIZATION" to evaluate errors in thinking and false mental patterns concerning spiritual values of worship and their corresponding scriptures*
- ❖ *Use spiritual valorization to evaluate uplifting Christ-centered verses on spiritual identity*

PART VIII
THE BALANCE OF CONSCIOUSNESS

35

MAINTAINING SPIRITUAL BALANCE

The ultimate goal of true spiritual consciousness is the balance of understanding true worship, the true Word, and true worth.

According to *Merriam-Webster's*, the word, "balance," is described as, "stability produced by an even distribution of weight on each side of a vertical axis; an equilibrium."

Balance is considered to be a healthy stabilizing aspect of physical fitness programs. Sports trainers and physical therapists repeatedly stress the need for balancing exercises as part of weight, strength, aerobic, and resistance training so as to prevent injuries.

In the world, we constantly are encouraged to maintain a balanced life. I have heard platitudes such as: We need to balance our work and play. Balancing our family and job is important. We have to learn to successfully juggle different aspects of our lives.

Balance has been used psychologically to describe mental and emotional stability. "Chemical imbalance" is a condition in which chemicals between the brain's nerve cells or "neurotransmitters" are off balance. This type of imbalance has been used to explain some anxiety and mood disorders. Politically, a "balance of power" has been defined as: "an equilibrium of power sufficient to discourage or prevent one nation or party from imposing its will upon or interfering with the interests of another." The world often refers to balance in legal or political terms, such as, the "scales of justice" and the "system of checks and balances." By societal, psychological, scientific, and political standards, the idea of balance appears to be a worthy endeavor. Most people seem to agree that too much of anything is a bad thing.

The Bible supports the reality that the only true balance is spiritual.

What does the Word of God concerning Christ say about "balanced"? Jesus encouraged those, who labor and are heavy-laden, to take his "yoke" upon them.

> Matthew 11:28-30:
> Come unto me, all ye that labour and are heavy laden, and I will give you rest.
> Take my yoke upon you, and learn of me; for I am meek and lowly in heart: and ye shall find rest to your souls.
> For my yoke is easy, and my burden [load] is light.

The term, "yoke," is the Greek word, ***zugos***, which means, "balance." When we are yoked or "balanced" with the master, Jesus Christ our Lord, we shall find rest.

The only real balance in life is to be balanced with Christ. He keeps us harmonious in all categories of body, soul, and spirit. Believers in Christ are "complete in him, which [who] is the head of [over] all principality and power" (Col. 2:10). A spiritually balanced life is to be attached, as a member of the One Body of Christ, to the Head of the Church, who is Christ.

Ephesians 4:15-16:

But speaking the truth in love, may grow up in him in all things, which is the Head, even Christ:

From whom [Christ] the whole body [all of the members of the One spiritual Body of Christ] fitly joined together and compacted by that which every joint supplieth, according to the effectual working in the measure of every part, maketh increase of the body unto the edifying of itself in love.

Colossians 2:19:

...holding the Head [Christ], from which all of the Body [members of the One Body of Christ] by joints and bands having nourishment ministered, and knit together, increaseth with the increase of God.

By being balanced with and attached to Christ the Lord, every member of the Body of Christ receives guidance for living. Christ is the handler of every *crisis* for all, particularly for those who believe in him.

In II Timothy, Chapter 1, the Apostle Paul described a delicate balance of spiritual power, spiritual love, and a spiritually sound mind, as a way to counteract ungodly cowardice, fear, and lack of valor.

Verse 7:

For God hath not given us [spiritual man] the spirit of fear [cowardice; weakened spiritual valor]; but [the spirit] of power, and [the spirit] of love, and [the spirit] of a sound mind.

Although balance is only available with God and His Son, Jesus Christ, he also stressed that we cannot balance our service to God and the world at the same time.

> Matthew 6:24:
> No man can serve two masters: for either he will hate the one, and love the other; or else he will hold to the one, and despise the other. Ye cannot serve God and mammon.

God discourages us from maintaining a "false balance" with the "god of this world," which influences worldly thoughts, systems, values and habit patterns.

> II Corinthians 4:3-4:
> But if our gospel be hid, it is hid to them that are lost:
> In whom the god of this world hath blinded the minds of them which believe not, lest the light of the glorious gospel of Christ, who is the image of God, should shine unto them.

The values of the world are sharply contrasted with spiritual values concerning Christ. Paul exhorted believers neither to be overly invested with the world nor to be unequally balanced with unbelievers in Christ.

> II Corinthians 6:14-15:
> Be ye not unequally yoked [unequally balanced] together with unbelievers: for what fellowship [balance] hath righteousness [the righteousness of God] with unrighteousness [the unrighteousness of the world]? and what communion hath light with darkness?
> And what concord hath Christ with Belial [world; works of the devil] or what part hath he that believeth

with an infidel [one who does not believe in or rejects Christ, as Son of God, savior, and lord].

Galatians 5:1:
Stand fast in the liberty wherewith Christ hath made us free, and be not entangled again with the yoke [balance] of bondage.

We are not to get caught up again with the world. We are not to try to balance the world with the Word of God concerning Christ. Materiality and spirit do not mix and cannot co-exist together.

Balance or over-balance with the world (i.e., reliance on self-works, worldly values, the law, and religiosity) is a "false balance of bondage."

Balance with Christ is liberty and freedom from mental bondage.

Galatians 5:6:
For in Jesus Christ neither circumcision [fleshly works; works of the world] availeth anything [have no value or weight], nor uncircumcision; but faith which worketh by love.

After we come to Christ, errors in thinking still can deceive us. Through subtle or overt pressure or pleasure from the world and its adversaries, we may misconstrue our valueness in Christ and pursue different types of unprofitable balances or imbalances of values.

36

DECEPTIONS AND BALANCES

Three Deceptions of Balance:

There are "three scenarios" that can deceive spiritual man into becoming more interested in worldly values and less interested in Christ. These scenarios also apply to unbelieving mortal men.

Deceptive Scenario #1: To feel or make himself more valued by the world, a believer in Christ deceives himself or is deceived into thinking that he needs to maintain a "balance of values" between Christ and the world. He is afraid of being perceived by the world as a fanatic religious.

Deceptive Scenario #2: In order to feel or make himself valued to the world, a believer consciously or unconsciously deceives himself or is deceived into shifting to a mental imbalance of values toward the world. This scenario would be characteristic of all unbelievers who do not know, believe, or reject Christ.

Deceptive Scenario #3: In order to feel or make himself worthy, a believer deceives himself into doubting or questioning his spiritual valueness and stand on the Word. As a result, he may become spiritually out of tune and can face perceived external or internal natural crises of God.

True balance is spiritual. It is only available within the spiritual realm through an ongoing fellowship with God and His Son, Jesus Christ, the Word, and The Holy Spirit.

There are Five Spiritual Balance Types:

Type/1: Balance of the full Word of God concerning the Christ: Spiritual man pursues rigorous spiritual knowledge of the prophecies of Christ's birth, his life, crucifixion, resurrection, ascension, the coming of 'The Comforter" (Holy Spirit) and the return of Christ. These realities are found in the Old Testament, the four Gospels, all of the Church Epistles, and the Book of Revelation.

Type/2: Balance of spiritual power, love, and a sound mind: Spiritual man hungers to sustain the three-fold balance of operating the manifestations of Holy Spirit, evidencing the love of God, and living the Word of God. II Timothy 1:7 states, "For God hath not given us the spirit of fear [cowardice]; but of power, and of love, and of a sound mind."

Type/3: Balance of "willing" and "doing" what God says to do: This balance includes spiritual hearing and doing the Word of God. Philippians 2:13 states, "For it is God which worketh in you both to will and to do of His good pleasure." James 1:22 states, "But be ye doers of the word, and not hearers only, deceiving your own selves."

Type/4: Balance of God's willingness and ability. God is always "willing and able" to help us, heal us, love us, and to provide a way out to escape any real or perceived conflict.

Type/5: Balance of spiritual consciousness concerning worship through the true Word and true worth. Spiritual man negates a *crisis* by continued growth in the understanding of how to worship the One true God, how to explore a spiritual understanding of His Word, and how to value man's divine nature and identity.

This last, but not least, balance highlights the spiritual purpose, thrust and direction of this book, *Escaping Spiritual Oblivion*. Spiritual consciousness of God is the major key to all wellbeing. An awareness of what we worship, to what degree, and how spiritual this worship is, will propel us to heightened purposefulness and contentment in our lives. A spiritual sense of the accuracy and integrity of God's Word, and how it unfolds the power and strength of our divine nature will allow us to soar to heights unknown.

For spiritual man, he is already in the "heavenlies" looking down at the problems or perceived conflicts of life.

> Ephesians 2:6-7:
> And hath raised us up together, and made us sit together in heavenly places in Christ Jesus:
> That in the ages to come he might show the exceeding riches of his grace, in his kindness toward us, through Christ Jesus.

EPILOGUE

Proverbs 23:7(a):

    For as he thinketh in his heart, so is he.

Mathew 6:21:

    For where your treasure is, there will your heart be also.

The values we uphold are related to the critical conditions we face. In this book, I focused on the spiritual cause and effect of man's perceived human crises. The biblical Greek word, *crisis,* was researched to describe in detail the underlying nature of, type of, and solution to spiritually based crises.

> *Spiritual oblivion is a disruption in spiritual values, in which mortal man lacks spiritual consciousness of God and errs in thinking regarding three spiritual areas: worship, the Word of God and one's inherent worth.*

In the natural realm, the fields of philosophy, psychology and "so-called" science have also explored these three areas. However, their definition, subtypes, interpretations and interventions usually are a counterfeit of the spiritual.

Issues of Worship

The world recognizes that greatly valuing (worshipping) something could be helpful or harmful. The helping professions willingly explore what you worship from a worldly, social, and even religious point of view. They explore people, places and things that you may over-value. This includes self, money, health, and recognition. The responses of secular or even religious clinicians, however, are to pursue issues within the individual, issues concerning others, and outside critical factors. The world would not deny that worship could be a problem. However, few if any professionals pursue the spiritual causes and effects of mistaken worship and the lack of spiritual consciousness a person has or may have regarding worship. Limited studies explore the possible underlying spiritual cause/effect of a person worshipping something more than or instead of Almighty God.

The professional world may assert that a person has made his health a god or her husband her god. These are considered destructive to individual self-esteem and growth. In the area of religion, it might be felt that a person's strong religiosity is too legalistic and judgmental resulting in critical conditions. Rarely, will a clinician instruct or provide information regarding a person's consciousness of his relationship to God as the only one to be greatly worshipped in spirit and in truth.

Issues of the True Word

In considering the value of words in understanding an individual's critical situation, the world will propound the need for communications skills. Clinicians use philosophy, self-help tools, theories, science, and physiology to explain underlying motives for words and the wisdom of words. The world relies heavily on the words of famous people and their expertise in specific areas to help understand and solve a crisis. Rarely does a professional provide biblical information or a choice to pursue spirituality through the Bible. When a client of mine went to a psychiatrist years ago, she warmly shared her love for God. His response was to claim that religion is a crutch and ended his comments by saying, "There is no God." Most people in crisis hardly think of spiritual direction nor are they provided with any. A caring counselor's values and attitudes toward worship and the Word of God will directly affect the spiritual outcome and future happiness for the client. Clients may need to be encouraged to consider Bible study or fellowship with people who love God. At least, they should know that there may be and usually are spiritual reasons for their present tormenting conditions.

Issues of True Worth

Mental health professionals, self-help groups, and personal coach training have focused on the importance of self-esteem and self-worth. Anxiety stemming from condemnation, guilt, narcissism, pride, and distorted relationships has brought many a client to the therapeutic setting to build him up or clarify his so-called "true" sense of self and wellbeing. In the spiritual realm, the only esteem that is to be greatly valued is God and how He values us. He loved us first. Therefore, we can love others as He in Christ loved us.

As spiritual man graciously grows in heightened spiritual consciousness of true worship, God's Word, and his inherent divine nature, he will realize that there is no real worldly crisis or spiritually based *crisis*. He takes a stand on God's truth, power, and love and refuses to be distracted by the world's view of crises and their solutions.

> Psalm 37:4-5:
> Delight thyself also in the Lord: and he shall give thee the desires of thine heart.
> Commit thy way unto the Lord; trust also in him; and he shall bring it to pass.

APPENDIX A

Mortal Man's Spiritual Oblivion

"Because matter has no consciousness or Ego, it cannot act; its conditions are illusions, and these false conditions are the source of all seeming sickness. Admit the existence of matter, and you admit that mortality (and therefore disease) has a foundation in fact. Deny the existence of matter, and you can destroy the belief in material conditions. When fear disappears, the foundation of disease is gone." Excerpt From: Mary Baker Eddy. "Science and Health with Key to the Scriptures (Authorized Edition)." Apple Books. https://books.apple.com/us/book/science-and-health-with-key-to-the/id441922830

There is a natural, materialistic world and a spiritual world. One is real and the other is unreal. You cannot combine the two. A serious error in thinking is to accept that both worlds can be mixed together and are equally important in handling critical conditions.

John 3:6:
That which is born of the flesh is flesh; and that which is born of the Spirit is spirit.

Galatians 5:17:
For the flesh lusteth against the Spirit, and the Spirit against the flesh: and these are contrary the one to the other: so that ye cannot do the things that ye would.

For natural or mortal man, a crisis is a difficult turning point that all will perceive or experience. It includes all human internal and/or external conditions that natural "five-senses" man may face. These circumstances solely are related to the things of the material world. A natural crisis is not limited to what the professional world defines as natural disasters or falsely so-called "acts of god."

In the world of humans, animals, vegetation and scientific data, there are a wide range of natural crises. These "so-called" worldly crises often involve circumstances outside of and/or within the individual or group such as, loss, illness, distorted relationships, financial hardships, changes in workplace/home environments, disasters and catastrophes. These reported critical conditions continue to be viewed and accepted as truth in communities, countries, and globally, even though man's heightened spiritual consciousness may negate these pseudo realities.

In the spiritual realm, *spiritual oblivion* differs from a natural crisis. It derives from a lack of spiritual consciousness concerning true worship.

A spiritual *crisis* is always the cause and effect of perceived natural crises. When "natural (mortal) man" consistently gives more value to the world than to spiritual matters, *oblivion* continues to disrupt his lifestyle, ultimately leading to inner or outer natural crises. Since he has NO spiritual understanding of true worship, the Word of God or his divine nature, this spiritual *crisis* persists, regardless of whether or not it is manifested in the natural world.

> 1 Corinthians 2:14:
> But the natural man receiveth not the things of the Spirit of God: for they are foolishness unto him: neither can he know them, because they are spiritually discerned.

For "spiritual man" who has a growing consciousness of true worship, the Word, and his spiritual worth, a natural crisis from within or without could lead to a spiritual *crisis, ONLY IF* he becomes distracted and begins to accept the worldly meaning and presence of a crisis. He starts to entertain worldly errors in thinking, unnecessary fears, and false values concerning God's ever-present truth and love.

> *There is a definite relationship between perceived*
> *physical, emotional, interpersonal, and/or intrapersonal*
> *natural crises and man's underlying spiritual oblivion.*

Because mortal or natural man does not know enough to spiritually understand or simply refuses to explore true worship or the Scriptures, he remains in *spiritual oblivion*. Even though he may follow religious rules and rituals, he is not aware of true fellowship with God through Christ. He does not feel that anything is missing in his life. In his natural reality, he has everything and has no apparent problem. This is the most spiritually dangerous condition to experience, because natural man sees himself as self-sufficient and without the need for God. As a result, he may not see the need for help or spiritual guidance from others.

Because of pressures and/or pleasures by people, places and things, mortal man continues to be deceived (as he had been since his experiences reported in Genesis, Chapter Two). He maintains false and flawed worldly values more than value toward God. Realizing it or not, this well-meaning and loving individual is giving supreme value to and worshipping certain aspects of the world (self, others, nature, attitudes) more than God.

Mortal man may not experience an obvious internal or external crisis. On the surface, he seems to himself and others to be doing okay. In fact, he may seem happier than a spiritually minded believer who is endeavoring to consistently stand on the Word of God. He cannot discover or verbalize an overt problem, but he may sense that something is wrong. Consequently, he may feel confused as to the nature of recent circumstances and sudden conflicts.

Because of his lack of spiritual consciousness and understanding of God and His Word, mortal man is left vulnerable to the onslaught of the world. He has no spiritual armor to protect himself. He values answers from the world instead of God. He is in *crisis* but does not know or comprehend it. When he experiences a natural crisis, this man may or may not seek help from family, friends and other worldly support systems. He will not consider pursuit of a spiritual counselor, another believer or a minister in a church, unless he has contact in his day-to-day life with someone who loves God and can offer advice.

In this materialistic world, mortal man will consistently break fellowship with God by his chronic errors in thinking and/or by knowingly or unknowingly worshipping and giving greater value, passion, and attention to the world. He either refuses to accept or lacks awareness that his critical condition has a spiritual cause related to the *worship of God*, through distorted thinking and understanding of His *Word* and a misunderstanding of the inherent worth of man. His flawed thinking or misinformation from worldly sources keeps him in *oblivion*. Because he will remain emotionally vulnerable, his poor choices and decisions can and probably will lead to one or more unfortunate natural crises.

REFERENCES

Works by the Author:

Cosenza, A.B. (2006). *Crisis intervention/Christ-is intervention*, Vol. I. Lincoln, NB: I-universe.

Cosenza, A.B. (2007). *Spiritual fitness training in valor: Crisis intervention/ Christ-is intervention, Vol. II.* Lincoln, NB: I-universe.

Cosenza, A.B. (2008). *Covalent counsel:* In pursuit of the ultimate intimate spiritual experience. Bloomington, IN: I-universe.

Cosenza, A.B. (2009). *By love convicted.* Bloomington, IN: I-universe.

Cosenza, A.B. (2020). *w.w.w.krisis/intervention.* Bloomington, IN: I-universe

Cosenza, A.B. (2022). *The Christ confidant mindset.* Bloomington, IN: I-universe.

Biblical:

American Heritage Dictionary. (2000). Wilmington: Houghton-Mifflin.

Eddy, Mary Baker G. (1906). Science and Health with Keys to the Scriptures. Mass: Christian Board.

King James Version of The Bible. (2001). Nashville: Thomas Nelson Inc.

King James Version Large Print Compact Bible. (2000). Nashville: Holman.

Merriam-Webster's New Collegiate Dictionary. (2002). Springfield: G. & C. Merriam.

The Oxford American Dictionary and Thesaurus. (2003). New York: Oxford University Press.

Young's Analytical Concordance to the Bible. (1970). Grand Rapids, Michigan: Eerdmans.

General Journal References:

Mary Baker Eddy. "Science and Health with Key to the Scriptures (Authorized Edition)." Apple Books. https://books.apple.com/us/book/science-and-health-with-key-to-the/id441922830

Hodge, D. R. (2013). Assessing spirituality and religion in the context of counseling and psychotherapy. In K. I. Pargament (Ed.) *APA Handbook of psychology, religion, and spirituality: Vol. 2. An applied psychology of religion and spirituality.* (pp. 93-123). Doi: 10.1037/14046-005

Paukert, A. L., Phillips, L. L., Cully, J. A., Romero, C. & Stanley, M. A. (2011). Systematic review of the effects of religion-accommodative psychotherapy for depression and anxiety. *Journal of Contemporary Psychotherapy, 41,* 99-108. Doi 10.1007/s10879-010-9154-0

Seeley P.S. (1955). Christian Science: The Healing Power of True Consciousness

C.S.B., of Portland, Oregon Member of the Board of Lectureship of The Mother Church, The First Church of Christ, Scientist, in Boston, Massachusetts. [Published in The Milwaukee County News of Milwaukee, Wisconsin, Dec. 1]

Worthington, E. L., Hook, J. N., Davis, D. E., & McDaniel, M. A. (2011). Religion and spirituality. *Journal of Clinical Psychology: In Session, 67,* 204-214. Doi: 10.1002/jclp.20760

Consciousness:

Akhtar, S. (2013). On Freud: the unconscious. New York: Routeledge Publishing

Chalmers, D. (1997). The conscious mind: In search of a fundamental theory. New York: Oxford Univ. Press.

Hawkin, D.R (2016). Transcending the levels of consciousness series: The stairway to enlightenment. Sedona: Veritas Publishing.

Seth, Anil (2021). Being You: A new science of consciousness. NYC: Dutton.

Harris, Annaka (2019). A guide to the fundamental mystery of the mind. New York: HarperCollins.

Koch, C. (2019). The feeling of life itself. Cambridge, Mass: MIT Press.

Ostojic, A. (2019). End of Oblivion: The Great Deception and why we need to reclaim our spiritual evolution. CA: Velton Publishing

Paulsen, N. (2002). The Christ consciousness. California: Sunburst Sanctuary.

Rowlands, M. (2001), The nature of consciousness. New York: Cambridge University Press.

Tolle, E. (1999). The power of now. Canada: Namaste Press.

Donald, Merlin. (2001) A mind so rare: The evolution of human consciousness, (First Ed). NY: W.W. Norton.

Crisis:

Caplan, G. (1964). Principles of preventive psychiatry. New York: Basic Books.

Golan, Naomi. (1978). Treatment in crisis situations. New York: Free Press.

James, R.K., Gilliland, B.E. (2017) Crisis intervention strategies. Boston: Cengage.

Yaeger K., Roberts, A.R. (eds.) (2015). Crisis intervention handbook. 4th edition, New York: Oxford University Press.

Printed in the United States
by Baker & Taylor Publisher Services